Twice in a Lifetime— and Then Some

A ZEST FOR LIFE

VEE Q

Twice in a Lifetime, and Then Some—
A Zest for Life

Copyright © 2022 by Vee Q

Paperback ISBN: 978-1-63812-472-6
Ebook ISBN: 978-1-63812-473-3
Hardback ISBN: 978-1-63812-484-9

All rights reserved. No part in this book may be produced and transmitted in any form or by any means, electronic, or mechanical, including photocopying, recording, or by any information storage and retrieval system, without permission in writing from the copyright owner.

The views expressed in this work are solely those of the author and do not necessarily reflect the views of the publisher hereby disclaims any responsibility for them. Published by Pen Culture Solutions 08/21/2022

Pen Culture Solutions
1-888-727-7204 (USA)
1-800-950-458 (Australia)
support@penculturesolutions.com

Twice in a Lifetime, and Then Some

A Zest for Life

In order to survive life and its many challenges, I believe we must expect the unexpected, meet the obstacles and overcome them by implementing carefully thought-out solutions, and embracing purpose, humor or amusement when opportunity affords.

Vee Q

Contents

Dedication..2
Preface..5
Introduction..8

Part One: Overcoming Life's Obstacles

Chapter 1	The Recurrence..12
Chapter 2	To Begin and Early On..18
Chapter 3	Coast to Coast...25
Chapter 4	Return to the Scene of the Crime..............................30
Chapter 5	Beautiful Lisbon, A Crossroad Between Moroccan and European Influence........................37
Chapter 6	A Very Anxious and Agonizing Return Trip from Portugal to Venice; Winding Down in Venice.....43
Chapter 7	Return to the United States after Six-Month European Experience; Settling Back Home in the United States..46
Chapter 8	Homeward Bound..50
Chapter 9	Daydreaming—Keep On Truckin'...........................54
Chapter 10	New York City, The Big Apple — A Glimpse into a City Like No Other; Settling into a New Life..57
Chapter 11	New York City Parking Rules: Alternate Sides Cleaning..63

Chapter 12	A Look into the Life of a New York City Market Vendor.................................67
Chapter 13	An Unbelievably Stupid Move.................................71
Chapter 14	Early Cruising with "Bella"....................................75
Chapter 15	Almost Meeting Elvis...78
Chapter 16	Third Time Is Not a Charm!..................................81
Chapter 17	A Perplexing, Extraordinary Experience..............84
Chapter 18	Life Goes On beyond Bumps and Grinds.............86
Chapter 19	The Battle of Excruciating Effects of Rheumatoid Arthritis (RA)....................................87
Chapter 20	Sharing Thoughts from My Introspection............90
Chapter 21	About Traveling, Vacations, and Dealing with Adversity..92
Chapter 22	Winter Travels from the East Coast to the West Coast...95
Chapter 23	Turning a Negative into a Positive: A Flight Cancellation in Nashville Becomes a Positive Experience...100
Chapter 24	Fabulous Solo Birthday Holiday: New York City–New Orleans (French Quarter) and Return...............................105
Chapter 25	An Enchanted Island Vacation with a Whopping Ending..113

Part Two: Very Personal Chapters and Expression of Deep Sentiments

Chapter 26	Cruisin' Cruisin'..121
Chapter 27	About Gordy..129
Chapter 28	The Closing of a Famous, Landmark Deli (and a Memoir of Ted)...............139
Chapter 29	Analogy of Life and Death..................................144
Chapter 30	Philosophies and Inner Thoughts (and Loss of Loved Ones).......................................147

Dedication

To my mother, whom I miss dearly, and to my sister, Val, who has always been by my side and supportive and instrumental in helping me through both of my cancers and other traumatic experiences; to Bella, my dearest friend, who was supportive and helpful through my second cancer experience; to my matriarch aunt, who herself was a victim of breast cancer, which resulted in a mastectomy, and who was very supportive through my second cancer experience; To Tim and Dean, the two men in my life who were both extremely supportive through my two experiences of cancer and who, because they showed no loss of love or desire for me despite these cancers, helped me to mentally recover with no residuals; and to all my family: Kay, Ted, Max, Jim, Poppy, Lana, Bob, Gordy, Kyle, and Bart, who were and have been supportive and caring throughout these experiences. To Eric, Gina and Rita, three of my dearest friends, who have been supportive throughout my life in New York, and to Merrill, in whose house I stayed following my mastectomy, for their support and kindnesses during my cancers and various traumatic experiences.

I'd also like to acknowledge my nephew and nieces—Vic, Darla, and Jean—who were very young when I had my cancer experiences. And I also acknowledge Jody, who had a very short marriage to my dearly beloved brother Ted, which ended in Ted's untimely death just a short nine months after their marriage and less than one month after their beautiful wedding ceremony.

My love and thanks go to each and all of them for their caring and support. And to my doctors—Drs. Yeager, Grayson, and Johns—who were professional and very supportive through my cancer treatments.

I thank my wonderful parents, John and Alicia, now deceased, who instilled in me and my siblings important character-building traits, such as honesty, compassion, and empathy for others, and an appreciation for hard work and its rewards—characteristics that are common among us siblings.

* * * * *

I honor my mother and father here by sharing with you their unbelievable bravery and heroism displayed in the face of enemy warfare during World War II. They both experienced unimaginable, harrowing, life-threatening hardships during this period.

My father was a sergeant in the US Army when the Japanese stormed the shores near Manila in the Philippines and took control of Bataan after hard-fought warfare. My father was one of thousands of soldiers taken prisoner and subsequently made to march in the infamous Bataan Death March, where they marched toward their firing squads. My father, in the face of this horrendous death threat, watched for and finally saw an opportune moment, when the guards turned away, to slip away from the march and hide quietly among the bushes. By the grace of God, he was not spotted by any of the guards. He was able to hide undetected among bushes until the march had passed. He then removed his military clothing and stripped down to his underwear, and under cover of darkness he carefully made his way to where my mother was staying.

He hid under the house, and as anticipated, Japanese soldiers came looking for him and confronted my mother. My mother, who was then eight and a half months pregnant, was terrified, but nonetheless displayed unwavering forethought, bravery, and courage; she stood firm to the Japanese soldiers as they threateningly wielded their weapons while searching the house. With all the courage she could muster, she defiantly denied having seen my father or having any knowledge of his whereabouts. Finally, satisfied that my father was nowhere in or near the house, they left my mother, whose only companion was my oldest brother, Jim, two years old at the time.

Later, when the Japanese were coming to overtake the village, my pregnant mother, with her two-year-old son in tow, escaped to the mountains, fearfully moving from cave to cave to escape Japanese soldiers looking for civilians. It was here in the mountains next to a river where my mother gave birth to my sister.

My heart swells with pride at the thought of my parents' focused thinking, bravery, and courageous actions in the face of terror. I'm thankful that they were able to function as they did and that they lived to pass on some of their qualities—namely, the ability to focus and think clearly in the face of danger and adversity. And I am very thankful that they were able to pass on to their offspring character-building traits of honesty, compassion, and empathy for others.

Preface

My inspiration to write this book began solidifying around the year 2000 after I recovered from my second bout with cancer in the right breast. I'd first been diagnosed with cancer nine years earlier, which required a lumpectomy and nineteen weeks of daily radiation. Cancer recurred in the same breast about seven years later. A mastectomy surgery ensued, which brought about my reliving all the painful emotions and anxieties with having to face that experience again. Then my resolve to write about my experiences was further encouraged when I was diagnosed with rheumatoid arthritis and also felt the horrible experience of shingles. At that point, I enhanced the title of my book from "Twice in a Lifetime" to "Twice In a Lifetime, and Then Some".

As I was going through my first bout with cancer, all the literature I could get my hands on were very clinical materials I had gathered from waiting rooms of hospitals, libraries, and various cancer agencies. Of course, these materials were very informative and needed to be reviewed for me to understand what I was going through and to learn about cancer—and my cancer in particular. However, I was already in a depressed state of mind and longed to get my hands on some light reading material that would be more inspirational and practical. When one is faced with a serious illness, that knowledge and realization is always foremost in the mind, one lives and experiences it 24/7. It is not necessary to read exclusively about the illness. Much of the time, patients affected by illness may welcome more inspiring reading material of true experiences of survivors who could offer insight in dealing with the mortality, the stresses and the trauma; survivors who might express or explain how they overcame the fears while experiencing their illnesses, and what can be expected for the future once recovered from illness. Looking forward to again experiencing things I enjoy doing in life was very beneficial in inspiring me with renewed hope and determination to go forward.

After my second bout with cancer, I began to seriously pursue bringing to fruition things I had dreamed of doing while I was recovering. To lift my spirits, I began to plan trips and travel, a pastime I always had enjoyed. During various trips, I often encountered interruptions, frustrations, and other nuisances and obstructions that I would have to overcome to continue and enjoy my travels. After the first few instances, I learned that by not allowing the various obstacles to anger and adversely occupy my emotions for a lengthy period of time—that if I could learn to control and minimize the amount of time I would allow myself to be angry and frustrated—I could then pick up and continue with my trips, putting the untoward incidents behind me and *out of mind*. This learning to control my anger and frustration was a difficult process, but eventually I was able to practice this with some ease. Often, I would even find a way to offset or turn that negative incident into a positive or to find some humor in the event. You will see some evidence of this practice in some of the chapters in this book.

Introduction

Life is like a stream flowing down a mountain. It flows over pebbles, reeds, twigs, rocks, and small branches as it continues on down the mountain. The river meanders downstream, hitting and flowing around the obstacles in its way. It comes across larger branches, larger rocks, and big logs and continues to circumvent them as it continues downstream. It hits larger tree trunks and small boulders and continues to flow around them and the myriad of obstructions as it continues its journey, flowing and meandering its way downward.

As in life, one must confront, circumvent or overcome the unending obstacles we all must encounter along life's journey.

When cancer reappeared seven years later, I was forced to dig deeper to bring out the strength to propel myself forward to overcome the agony of accepting the impending mastectomy. Decisions going forward would be more difficult than with the first occurrence since this time I had the added strain of planning my treatment and recovery with the financial hardship of no health insurance to aid in the burdensome costs.

With a later diagnosis of rheumatoid arthritis and then herpes zoster (shingles), there was seemingly a never-ending succession of health issues. Still later, a diagnosis of GCA (giant cell arteritis) resulted in a two-and-a-half or three-hour *awake* surgery with local anesthesia (an experience I hope to never again need). These were taxing challenges to my constitution and ability to continue to cope. Despite all, I developed, with much effort, an ability to maintain an upbeat, positive attitude. The truth is, despite my various ailments, I do consider myself, fortunately, quite healthy, as long as my weekly rheumatoid arthritis injections and other medications are controlling my ailments.

My philosophy in life is to plug along as best I can, despite the obstacles I have faced. I believe in this life we all have our share of pain, heartache, health issues, and disappointments. Life poses a myriad of obstacles, most unforeseen, unexpected, and untimely. In order to survive life and its many obstacles, I believe we must expect the unexpected. When it hits, take a deep breath and ponder it awhile to absorb the shock. When you've gathered your bearings, begin to assess the situation and form a solution. You may or may not wish to involve a close confidant outside of your family, one you respect who is a *good listener* who can be objective and *not too opinionated*, and who will patiently allow you to express your fears and concerns in order that you may reach your own independent conclusions. If the problem is health-related, obviously a health professional should be consulted. I was very fortunate through both of my cancer experiences to have very close confidants who allowed me to voice my fears, my thoughts and concerns, and basically just listened, offering their input only when it was sought. They allowed me to sort out my emotions and feelings in order that I could more readily accept my situation and see a way forward. This cleared the way for me to become more proactive in finding solutions to the situations confronting me.

* * * * *

I have focused my book more on looking forward from an illness, to a time of recovery and events of enjoyment once healed. For myself, during my treatment and healing period, I focused on a favorite pastime: travel and vacations.

Earlier in the book, I share my thoughts and analyses of how I dealt with the initial turmoil of hearing the devastating diagnosis that I had cancer. The fear, anxiety, emotional turmoil one feels when hearing of a serious illness diagnosis are difficult to adequately impart to another. Facing one's own mortality and all the feelings associated with hearing of a diagnosis of cancer or other serious illness can only truly be felt by the individual experiencing it. That is why I feel reading about true experiences of others both during and beyond treatment and illness can be very encouraging and uplifting.

Through this writing, I have shared my inner thoughts in dealing with various anxieties and some outcomes. Beyond offering insight and encouragement in dealing with illness, I have tried to keep this a light and entertaining read, with some stories offering a diversion from the gravity and seriousness of the subject at hand. Some stories hopefully will leave inspiration or a meaningful message with the reader; others may be just lighthearted, humorous and wholesome entertainment. Although many of the stories may seem overstated, enhanced or totally fabricated or seemingly untrue or unbelievable, the events are, in fact, as depicted. Particularly, post-cancer stories may exude a heightened sense of lightheartedness. As explained further in the book, my more seemingly uncaring, loose attitude about life in general stems from my survival of grave, serious illnesses. Through these stories, I hope to impart a hope and ever-renewing determination to move forward into an enlightened sense of appreciation for life and its rewards.

Part One
Overcoming Life's Obstacles

Life is but one quick visit in time; and time is precious.

With each fork in the road, with each obstacle, and at every turn, we must strive to take control of the situation. Unfortunately, we are often limited in time to make a decision as to which direction to take. By quickly and thoughtfully analyzing a situation and then going forward, one can lessen the stress of the circumstance at hand. Especially when encountering adverse health issues, one could easily feel totally helpless.

Regardless of the circumstance, overcoming the feeling of helplessness could strengthen your constitution and offer relief. This strengthening of oneself may be accomplished by making a concerted effort to quickly assess the circumstance and options available, and by going forth with the best, most thought-out decision for the optimum possible result. Once you have weighed your options and have made your informed decision, you may begin to experience relief and reduced anxiety because you have now gained control of your situation.

As to the many unforeseen, untoward circumstances that come across our lives, trying to minimize the time you allow to feel anger or frustration may relieve the stress and propel you forward with a more positive frame of mind. Finding humor when possible is an added dose of medicine.

When I have been successful in exercising these practices, the outcomes have left me with a more enlightened outlook going forward.

1
The Recurrence

Circa July 1998. It was a hot and very humid day in New York City in early July. As I sat in my eighth-floor apartment on the love seat in my den watching TV with the window behind me wide open, I happened to brush my hand along the side of my right breast and thought I felt a lump. As I felt around the right breast where I had had a lumpectomy and daily radiation treatments for nineteen weeks seven years earlier, I felt a small, roughly half-inch-wide bump. I began to become concerned as I self-examined my breast. I recently had my breasts examined and received what I believed was a clearance from my doctor; he had not seen any concerning findings. The next day, I made an appointment to return to the Cancer Center regarding the lump I had found. I subsequently was scheduled to have a biopsy taken of the lump the following week.

I returned to the Cancer Center and had the biopsy taken, after having a local anesthetic administered. During the biopsy, I thought the doctor gave her assistant an odd eye contact, but I dismissed it.

Having completed the procedure, I proceeded to go to work in our gift shop in Greenwich Village. Because it was not yet ten in the morning, the village was quiet since shops typically opened around noon and remained open for business until two o'clock the following morning. Since it was early and our workers had not yet arrived, I had to raise the heavy metal roll-up gate myself in order to open the front door. (At this point, I had not thought much about the biopsy procedure I had just completed.)

A few days later, I received a telephone call from my doctor, requesting that I come in to her office to review the findings of the biopsy. In our appointment, I was given the utterly upsetting news that the lump found in my breast was malignant and that the cancer in my right breast had returned, despite the nineteen weeks of daily radiation treatments I had had seven years earlier. My doctor counseled me that this time I needed to prepare to have a mastectomy; because this was a recurrence, a mastectomy would be the best recommended procedure in the interest of removing the entire cancer. Having my entire breast removed was an absolutely nauseating thought for me.

The emotional turmoil, the fear, and the terrifying experience of again facing my mortality were almost more profound than with my first cancer experience. The thought of actually losing my breast as opposed to treating and saving it was the most difficult and excruciating reality for me to accept. However, with possible reconstructive surgery, the physical appearance might not be too altered. There was another consideration, which paled against the gravity of again facing my mortality but nonetheless was an important issue with me. Apart from all the other terrifying considerations, I loved wearing colorful bras and matching colorful underwear, and I was quite sure that mastectomy bras were available only in what I considered to be colorless white. I preferred interesting and bright appealing colors in my wardrobe, since colors were more compatible with my skin tone. Also, I liked mixing and matching colors to enhance my moods and to put me in a better frame of mind. I abruptly realized that when pitted against all the other grave, serious realities, this concern was more of a nuisance and had no place for consideration at this point. At this juncture, there were other more serious and pressing issues to deal with.

This recurrence was far more difficult for me to confront than my first cancer experience because of, among other things, financial and insurance considerations. With the first cancer, I had good health insurance coverage. This time, I was a part owner in a small business, and we were unable to afford health insurance premiums. Therefore, I did not have any health insurance, and I would have to carry the burden of the entire cost of the mastectomy myself. I did not have the resources nor savings in the substantial amount needed for the surgery. I consulted with my doctor at the Cancer Center and advised her of my financial situation. The cost of surgery at the Cancer Center would be absolutely prohibitive without insurance and with my limited financial resources. She suggested that she had a colleague in Sacramento, California, where I happened to have had my last surgery, who probably could perform the mastectomy for me and who might be able to arrange to have the procedure performed in an outpatient clinic (same day surgery and discharge) in order to substantially reduce the cost.

So arrangements were made between my doctor and her colleague in Sacramento to perform my mastectomy in an outpatient clinic in Sacramento. Additionally, simultaneously with the mastectomy, a reconstructive surgeon would insert a breast implant to essentially match the size and shape of the noncancerous breast.

As with my first experience of studying and learning about my illness, I was again forced to focus exclusively on my illness, setting aside all other problems in order to direct all my energy and emotional stability to (1) accepting the fact that I again had cancer and (2) trying to calm my nerves and emotions so that I could focus all my attention to battling this illness that had returned to my body. I again needed to prioritize my energy and emotions in order to direct them to achieving these two goals. I had to accept the reality that I must first prepare myself emotionally for what lay ahead. Just as in accepting death, this was an emotional acceptance that I had to come to terms with alone.

I knew time was of the essence, so I began to take the necessary steps to proceed in an orderly, sensible manner. Since I had to return to Sacramento, California from my home in New York for my surgery, I made arrangements with my ex-husband, Tim, to stay in his home in Sacramento while he would be away on business immediately following my surgery, and to stay with my friend Merrill thereafter for a few days during my recovery. Roughly two weeks later, I flew to Sacramento for my surgery.

My sister and my aunt, who was a cancer/mastectomy survivor, met me at the airport, and we went to stay in my ex-husband's house for the night. To occupy my mind so as not to think too anxiously about my impending surgery, I decided to do some light cleaning around the house. I wondered and hoped that I would fully recover quickly and would soon be able to again do such chores.

We would return to Tim's house after my surgery for a few days before going on to Merrill's house for another couple of days of recovery time before heading back home.

Day of Surgery

On the day of my surgery, I was quite apprehensive as we drove into the parking lot of the little clinic where my surgery was to be performed. The clinic was housed in a small wooden bungalow in the midst of a rather large parking lot in a wooded area. It was a rustic, rather peaceful setting, which was in deep contrast to the emotional turmoil I was experiencing within. My surgeon greeted me soon after I had settled in and advised me that the reconstruction surgeon would arrive soon. Before long, I was administered anesthesia for the surgery. The surgery took about two and a half hours to complete. Following the surgery, I stayed in the recovery room for nearly two hours before being discharged to go home.

While I was in the recovery room, my surgeon gave me the disappointing news that the reconstruction part of my surgery had not been performed. My surgeon informed me that due to the nineteen weeks of daily radiation that I had had seven years earlier, my skin around the affected breast had lost its elasticity, and therefore the reconstructive surgeon was unable to complete the implant insertion and reconstruction. The obstacle was that with the insertion of the implant, the skin would not stretch to meet at the closure, resulting in the necessity to abort the immediate implant and reconstruction portion of the surgery. Needless to say, this added to my anxiety, but I would try to let that lie for now and think about it at a later time. Because of this development, there would be necessary, enormous considerations to address and complications and costs to weigh. Now was not the time to think about all that.

A Little Reflection Back to When I Was First Diagnosed with Cancer

After the radiation treatments and recovery from my first cancer, fortunately, I began to feel rather normal and actually did not think of myself as a cancer survivor, but rather a healthy person, capable of pursuing life to its fullest, emotionally and physically. As a matter of fact, when I would see my doctors for later examinations, they were quite amazed (amused?) at my "healthy" attitude.

However, this recurrence posed more trauma than the first instance of cancer because of the current financial considerations and now facing additional problems relative to having to abort and forgo the immediate, simultaneous implant/reconstruction portion of my surgery. Postponement of and later addressing that situation would prolong the time before I would finally be able to fully focus on recovery.

Assessing My Current Situation and Applying Thought Processes to Go Forward with a More Positive Outlook on Life

While recovering, I contacted the cancer center in Sacramento, where they fitted me for a breast form and mastectomy bras (as I feared, there were no bright-color bras available). I also met with a cancer/mastectomy survivor/counselor, who was very kind and consoling.

After about two weeks, I returned to New York City and resumed my normal life and work schedule. I sought comfort in my work, my family, my friends, faith, and loved ones.

In the ensuing months, I did some serious reflection, soul-searching, and planning for my strategy going forward. With much thoughtful consideration, I decided that the only way forward and the thing to do would be to learn to enjoy life again. I began to think more of traveling, a pastime I so enjoyed. I resolved to try to continue to focus and give the immediate, more serious and grave situations their proper attention, and to address the less imminent, less pressing circumstances in a more lighthearted but thoughtful, considerate, and responsible manner. I felt I should try very hard to look at life's daily challenging circumstances and experiences with a little humor when and if at all possible. I thought that by adopting this way of thinking, I would be more able to face whatever other obstacles lay ahead. In the years following this surgery, I have found that adopting this type of thought process has been very helpful to me.

2

To Begin and Early On

To begin my story, I reflect on my happy childhood, free and clear of the current mundane problems of daily stacks of mail with 60 percent junk (but you don't dare throw them out without first going through them to make sure none of your more important mail got stuck in the middle of all the junk mail); the problems of long grocery lines and long waits at the bus stops or on the subway platforms; and slow (deathly slow) sale days with sixty dollars in sales after three hours of greeting customers and helping them try on hats and jewelry. Oh, and I think of those "healthy" days as a youngster, free of cancer and rheumatoid arthritis and weekly medical injections, without the high blood pressure, weight gain, stubborn belly fat, and myriad of problems incidental to daily life as an adult.

I think of my early carefree childhood days—like at age five, riding on the ledge at the window above the back seat of a 1950s Nash while coming home from a family outing on "Buck Night" at the drive-in in Richmond, California. Again in Richmond, going to the drugstore with my sister to cash in a coupon for a clip-on plastic bird to decorate a Christmas tree.

Later, at age ten in San Francisco, taking the trolley with my sister to Powell Street to Woolworth's and getting a slice of pizza.

A little later, at age twelve, on Thanksgiving, me and my family (Mom; Dad; sister, Val; and three brothers; Jim, Max, and Ted) were getting ready to go to Golden Gate Park for a picnic with our turkey. My father, bless his soul, had a habit of "supervising" my mother and my sister in the kitchen, which he was doing today. My mother and sister got so frustrated with my father meddling in the kitchen that they finally shooed him out so they could take care of packing everything for the picnic in the park. Well, we finally got everything packed in the car, and off we went to Golden Gate Park. We unpacked all our goodies and condiments. But lo and behold, when we looked for the turkey, it was nowhere to be found; it still sat where we had forgotten it—in the oven in the kitchen at home! Needless to say, my father was extremely upset, but he won in the end, since thenceforth, my mother and sister could no longer shoo my father out of the kitchen!

I always loved going to Golden Gate Park for our family outings. We had many family picnics there; we'd also go there for our Easter egg hunts. Poor Dad, one Easter he hid the eggs—unfortunately among the poison oak. Oh my goodness—my poor father was riddled with hives that night, and my mom had to apply calamine lotion all over his body. That was an Easter to remember.

On another family outing in Golden Gate Park at about age twelve, I remember me and my brother Max (two years younger than I) were coming back from the bathrooms when I looked up and saw this huge "coconut" in a tree. I pointed it out to my brother, and we decided to get the coconut and take it back to the picnic. We began gathering and throwing rocks to knock the coconut down. No sooner had we thrown a rock apiece, when all of a sudden, bees were swarming all around us, and we ran for our lives. We never got our coconut but got instead a beehive full of bees and a bee sting or two. I still laugh about that every time I relive that story.

I come from a military family. Both my father and my brother Jim retired from the US Army, each with at least twenty years of military service. My brother Max served in the US Air Force in Vietnam, with short intermittent assignments in Thailand. We all have a high respect for those who've fulfilled their patriotic duty in service of our country.

Life, Love, and War

Later on, at the age of fifteen and a half, going to the drive-in on a Friday date was the thing to do for many of the teenagers in our school. I met Jake in high school and developed a mad crush on him. Jake was very good-looking: tall and slender, with dark hair and sideburns. When he wore his black leatherlike outfit, he reminded me very much of his idol, Elvis. To me, Jake was gorgeous. We'd often go to the movies—either walk-in or drive-in. Before going to the drive-in, I'd buy a huge loaf of French bread and slice it and butter the slices. I preferred this to popcorn. I loved to fix food for Jake. After school many days, I'd fix him grilled cheese sandwiches; he'd eat three or four at a time. Once, my father came in and saw that I was feeding Jake so many grilled cheese sandwiches, and he complained that I was feeding Jake so much of our food. My father was struggling to support a family of seven on a minimum-wage job. Of course, at the time I thought he was just being mean. I understand now and empathize with my father's dilemma at that time.

Jake and I dated for two and a half years; then at age eighteen, Jake received his draft notice. We were both very sad and apprehensive about the likelihood that he would be sent to Vietnam. We decided to get married before he went to boot camp. So with no witnesses, we went to the justice of the peace at City Hall in San Francisco and got married. Oh my God! His mom was livid. My parents, on the other hand, were quite fond of Jake and were pleased with our marriage. I think we got married the day before he was due to leave for boot camp.

Six weeks into his eight-week training at boot camp, Jake's mom, Sandy, and I went to visit him at Fort Ord near Monterey. Monterey is a lovely quaint seaside town, a great weekend retreat that Tim and I frequented on many weekends later on. Obviously, the boot camp was a little distance from the wharf and commercial areas, which were replete with restaurants, motels, and inns.

Sandy and I were quite entertained while watching the soldiers in formation, marching and singing as they marched. After listening and attempting several times to decipher the words of their songs and chants, I finally was able to understand: "Army—so good! Liquor—no good! Women—no good." We got a chuckle out of that.

It was a difficult, sad, and lonesome time for me after Jake went off to boot camp. For the past two and a half years, we had seen each other each and every day, with a possible day or so exception, if that. And now I was not only lonesome, but the apprehension of his going off to war in Vietnam was very heavy—with the possibility that he might never come home alive, as so many soldiers were dying there. A schoolmate, who became engaged prior to her fiancé going to Vietnam, lost her fiancé to the war. As he was parachuting down from the plane, he was shot down and killed by enemy fire. He was just a helpless, moving target. That story was too close to home for comfort. I felt thankful that Jake was in the artillery rather than the infantry. I wrote him every day, and he would write when he could, about once a week.

I believe it was about six or eight months after going to Vietnam that Jake got his R & R (rest and recuperation) leave. He and others were flown to Hawaii, and I met him there. Unfortunately, it never occurred to me to go to the base (Fort Drew) and meet him. I awaited him in the hotel. Our hotel balcony faced the street, and I was so excited when I thought I saw him get out of a cab. When he got to the room, he inquired why I didn't meet him at the base. All the other soldiers' wives met them there; Jake was the only one without a welcome party. I felt so bad that I hadn't thought to also be there.

Jake was discharged after two years' service in our US Army. The Jake I knew pre-military service was very different from the Jake who came home post-Vietnam. He would search out war movies on TV during the day, and I began to notice he was doing this when I was home as well on evenings and weekends. I became frightened when I watched his reactions to some of the combat scenes.

We fumbled along for about two years after he came back from Vietnam, and eventually we ended our marriage in divorce. I've often looked back with regret and thought that I should have been more supportive of Jake. Unfortunately, and most regrettably, I was just a young girl who was frightened and confused by the new Jake; too young to understand what he was going through. After all, he and many of the other soldiers with whom he served were drafted at the age of eighteen and in a period of weeks were sent to war to fight for our country.

The tragedy for those who fought in Vietnam was that, not only did those soldiers not get the homecoming welcome that other soldiers received from World War II, but upon their return home, the Vietnam soldiers were chastised and booed and berated for their part in fighting that war. I learned later that while in Vietnam, those soldiers had no idea of the dissension brewing in the United States for our participation in that war. The soldiers were shielded from newspaper articles and the like depicting the turmoil back home about US involvement. To them, while fighting, they were fulfilling their patriotic duty to their country. The travesty here was the shock many returning Vietnam soldiers felt upon returning home and being chastised or berated for their part in the war. As a rule, the antiwar activists and much of the public were insensitive to the sentiments of the returning soldiers, unwilling to acknowledge that these soldiers were willing to sacrifice their lives in patriotic duty and love of country. Returning soldiers slowly came to the realization that some of their fellow soldiers/brothers who had died in combat had sacrificed their lives in vain. Despite the fact that those soldiers had experienced the ultimate sacrifice of death in patriotic duty and for the good of the country, that country as a whole was thankless for those sacrifices. Many of these returning soldiers had gone to war as young as eighteen years of age. As young soldiers, they experienced incomparable sacrifices in surviving war and then returned to turmoil and dissension in the country regarding the war. Knowing their part in the war and what they had just experienced, one can only imagine the emotional trauma that many of them were feeling. I'm sad for those soldiers, for the fear, heartache, pain, and loss of comrades they experienced at war; and I'm full of sorrow at the thankless homecoming they received upon their return. I empathize with why many of them suffered postwar issues.

I, for one, feel that I was horribly negligent in not being more empathetic with Jake upon his return from Vietnam. Remorsefully, my age at the time did not afford me the years of experience needed to understand his situation and to encourage him to seek medical assistance in dealing with his adjustment to civilian life. I have not had the opportunity to express these thoughts to Jake, since sadly, I have had no communication with him since we divorced so many years ago.

Life Goes On

I think my best years in life after my happy childhood began in my midthirties. At this age, I was cancer-free, and this was a time when I feel life really began for me. I was at a point in life when I felt somewhat secure and quite free to do as I pleased. I had been separated from my second husband for two years. I felt it was time to begin living as I saw fit, without the constraints of marriage or having to account to another for my doings and whereabouts. Since I had tried desperately to keep my second marriage together through (at this time) two years of "temporary" separation and fruitless hopes of resuming marriage, I felt I had no alternative but to enjoy life. I suffered a near nervous breakdown trying to bring my marriage back together again, since I had sworn to myself that I would not go through another divorce. But finally, when I began feeling severely emotionally unstable and my entire nervous system began to feel very shaken and unstable, I accepted the fact that I could do no more to save this marriage; that marriage is a 50-50 or sometimes 60-40 share of control, and I had exhausted my 50 or 60 percent of control. Therefore, it was time to give up. I saw no other outlet. I could brood about my situation, but brooding in my mind was not a viable alternative. The only positive way forward and the thing to do would be to learn to enjoy life singly again, although I knew that would take extreme effort and a serious reassessment of my outlook on life and establishing future goals while maintaining my integrity.

This feeling of satisfying independence continued for about two years, until I was first diagnosed with cancer. At that point, I was thrown into a situation I had not encountered thus far in my life. I knew that in order to survive this dilemma, I had to search deep within myself to learn to accept my situation, find a solution, and go forth with whatever was necessary to overcome this issue. Hopefully, I would come out of the situation completely healed and ready to go forth with my life.

3

Coast to Coast
(Post-Cancer #1)

Eyeglasses sinking slowly out of sight into the Grand Canal in Venice became a good omen for a future return to Venice.

I feel a little more background might be appropriate here: I live in New York City, having moved here from Northern California (near the San Francisco Bay Area) in the fall of 1994. I had just returned from spending six months in Europe, visiting and enjoying many European cities and the beautiful artwork of master painters. The majority of the six months was spent in Venice, Italy, mostly enlightening and immersing myself in the local culture and daily living. I took daily rides on a *vaporetto* (ferry) along the bustling Grand Canal, passing the many mansions/palaces lining the canal in this beautiful, enchanting city.

How did this transition take place? Well, in the spring of 1993 my ex-husband offered me a coupon for a two-for-one airfare, so I invited a coworker/friend/drinking buddy to take a tour with me through Europe. Fran was a petite five feet two inches, blonde, with a cute pixie hairdo. She was very vivacious and spontaneous, with a fabulous sense of humor. Fran and I settled on a sixteen-day tour through Europe, after flying to London to meet the tour. We toured about ten countries, riding in our private bus with music playing (in different languages, including English) as we rode through the countrysides. It was an enjoyable ride as we went from city to city, stopping to tour the various cities and then retiring in the evenings for our overnight stay, usually in hotels just outside the city, with ready accessibility to town. Dinner was usually included, and five o'clock the next morning was the time to make sure your luggage was outside your door for pickup for the next day's ride. Usually, after Fran and I disembarked from the bus at the end of the day at the various hotels, we would head for the bar and have a drink (or two) before dinner. This was a two-week tour, and toward the end, Fran whispered to me that she was tired of many of our cotravelers following us into the bars and sitting with us at day's end. (Fran and I were two of the youngest of the group we were traveling with, and the others were amused at our energy and the fact that we had fun and laughed frequently, so they wanted to be around us.) So sometime in the second week, we decided to ditch our followers and race from the bus to the bar before they could follow.

Venice, Italy: We stayed in Mestre, just outside Venice near the train station. After dinner, a group of about five of us decided to go into Venice, where we took a *vaporetto* (ferry) ride along the Grand Canal. It was a beautiful night, with gondolas sharing the canal and intermittently passing alongside our *vaporetto*. Needless to say, all of us were very happy and having a fabulous time (aided by our consumption of glasses of wine at dinner). A passenger, who had been observing us having a great time, offered to take a picture of all of us. I decided to take my eyeglasses off for the photo op. I was holding my glasses in my hand as we all put our arms around one another's shoulders. *Then an incredulous, untoward accident happened: my eyeglasses slipped out of my hand and dropped right into the canal water.* In my drunken state, I leaned over the railing and stared with remorse and disbelief as I watched my glasses sink into the water and out of sight. *There went my brand-new $260 prescription glasses, worn only once, which I had purchased just before this trip!* I was absolutely sick! But, luckily, I had brought another pair of glasses, which I had back in the room, at the advice of one of my tour books that I had read before taking this trip.

(Thank God I took the advice of Trips to bring an extra pair of glasses along with me.)

Dear, sweet Fran consoled me: "Don't worry, Vee. That's a good omen." In her positive and joyous outlook, she said, "It just means that you will come back here someday, because you left your glasses here." She was right. I returned to live in Venice the following year for six months.

So we continued on our tour and headed south to Rome, where our trip would end. Upon our arrival in Rome, we disembarked the bus to check into our room. Then Fran and I headed down to the bar for our afternoon cocktails. Fran was a Scotch drinker, and she began enjoying her drinks. I, on the other hand, drank tequila gimlets. Fran had an incredible ability to hold her liquor and drank at least two and a half to three of one of my drinks. After about two hours, I suggested to Fran that we go elsewhere. Fran said she had found her spot, was very happy, and wasn't moving from her chair (and she meant it!). We ended up sitting in that lounge and drinking and drinking, believe it or not, for a total of about eleven hours. Finally, we decided to go find a restaurant and were joined by two other fellows who had been drinking with us at the bar. That was a marathon I will never forget! Our two-week trip ended when we flew back home to California the following day.

Speaking of flying, our flight to London had been a very uncomfortable, unhappy, and anxious trip for many of the passengers seated around us in the smoking section in the rear of the plane. (Keep in mind that, at this time, smoking was allowed on flights, both domestic and international, and the issue of smoking had not become the widespread resistance that it has become in the present day.) Fran and I had boarded the plane and were putting our luggage in the overhead compartment. One or two of the passengers lit cigarettes, and soon after, an announcement came over the speaker that this was being converted to a nonsmoking flight. Of course, the smokers sitting in the smoking section of the plane groaned in agony. There was no warning that this would be a nonsmoking flight prior to passengers boarding the plane. If there had been warning, the smoking passengers would have had their cigarettes before boarding the plane and would have mentally prepared themselves for not smoking for the next eight hours or so. It was explained by an airline hostess to the complaining smoking passengers that *because there was a nonsmoking passenger sitting in the smoking section of the plane who had complained of the smoke, the captain decided to honor the complaint of the nonsmoking passenger and made the entire roughly eight-hour flight a nonsmoking flight.* Needless to say, those of us smokers sitting in the smoking section were very upset, especially at not being warned prior to boarding that this would be a nonsmoking flight.

While I realize nonsmokers would hail this move, I know that smokers can well understand the frustration and anxiety that Fran, I, and other smokers experienced by this unexpected, unwarned infringement on what we expected to be a long, enjoyable, and comfortable flight.

4

Return to the Scene of the Crime (Post-Cancer #1)

I began to feel adventuresome, with a renewed curiosity to visit other parts of the world. For many years, I had longed to visit Europe. Now that I'd had a taste of the history, the ambiance, and the incredible abundance of art displayed throughout the towns and cities Fran and I visited on our two-week jaunt through Europe, my desire to see more was unleashed. Coupled with my post-cancer underlying urgency to experience as much and as soon as possible, I was ready for adventure and to travel and learn of life in a different culture.

After I returned home to California, I developed a strong desire to return to Venice. I began making plans to do so and decided to research the possibility of living in Venice for about six months. This required much planning, since I had been living very comfortably in my completely furnished three-bedroom, two-bath, two-car-garage home in the very desirable Greenpoint area of Sacramento. Additionally, I had recently purchased a brand-new Toyota GTS, which would have to be housed during my absence.

More importantly, I had an ailing mother in San Francisco who had suffered and continued to suffer ministrokes. Fortunately, we had four siblings living in the area, three of whom, including me, were charged with her twenty-four-hour care. I would have to arrange with my other siblings to take on the responsibility of my assigned care time for my mother.

I decided to pack and put all my belongings and all the contents of my house into storage and arrange for a property manager to rent my home in my absence. Thus, I began solidifying my plans. For the next six or seven months, I would slowly pack all my belongings. I cursed myself when I realized how foolishly I had accumulated so many items in the four years I had lived there—especially when I realized I had been frivolously accumulating items that *I couldn't live without while I was in a store shopping, but obviously lost the impulse when I returned home. I was annoyed when while packing, I found so many newly purchased, unused, unworn items containing price tags on them!* Imagine my frustration at the realization that this ridiculous practice was now costing me a much-increased burden in my quest to complete packing all my belongings.

Return to Venice, and More of Europe

As part of my plan to return to Venice for six months, I decided to learn to speak Italian so that I could better absorb the Italian culture. I went to a bookstore and was lucky to find an excellent and easily understood Italian language book, which I purchased. I decided that in the next six months, I would teach myself how to speak and basically understand the Italian language. Over the next six months, almost every single night I would sit up in bed and study this book at least a few minutes before retiring. The most difficult element of the language for me to overcome was the pronunciation of the combined characters *ch*, which in English is more of a soft *c* sound, but in Italian it is the sound of the letter *k*. Once I was able to master that difference in the two languages, it became easier for me to learn Italian. As a consequence, when I finally did consummate my dream to return to Venice, I was well armed to basically understand someone speaking to me in Italian, and I was able to make myself understood to that person. When I went to restaurants, I ordered in Italian, but rather amusing to me was that the waiter/waitress would frequently respond to me in English. I became friendly with some of the waiters/waitresses who came to know me. They often asked if I was a teacher, since apparently I spoke quite well in their language. Many of them were happy to practice their English with me.

Once I went to the post office while visiting the Lido in Venice on one of my day jaunts. I waited in line, and when it came to my turn, I stepped up, and a man farther behind me in line also stepped up; he had intended to help me relay my request to the teller, as it was obvious to him that I was not a local and might have difficulty conveying my request. I put my hand up to stop him and thanked him in Italian for his kindness, but I felt I would be perfectly capable of communicating my request to the teller. He stepped back in awe and listened to me while I conveyed my order to the teller, requesting airmail posts to the United States for my postcards. As I left the post office, I again thanked the kind gentleman, and he responded and smiled.

If you are unfamiliar with Venice, you may not know that there are no vehicles allowed to operate along the cobblestone streets of Venice. The mode of transportation in Venice is by *vaporetto* (a small ferry-type boat) or by foot. I had learned that I could get a local *vaporetto* pass for the time I was staying in Venice, since I planned to reside there for six months. Consequently, I was able to minimize the costs of my daily *vaporetto* rides. During my stay in Venice, along with visiting many churches that housed beautiful artworks of all the various masters, such as Michelangelo, Botticelli, Rafael, Tintoretto, and so many more, I would take a ride on a *vaporetto* every day, usually along the Grand Canal from the Saint Marks Square area, where my various hotels were located, to the train station. Sometimes I would walk back from the train station to my hotel (not a short distance, I might add), stopping to visit various museums, churches, or palaces along the way. Other times I would take a round-trip ride on a *vaporetto* to the Lido, located across the Grand Canal from Saint Marks Square. I frequently enjoyed a morning *vaporetto* ride to the Lido to enjoy a quiet breakfast away from the hustle and bustle of the Saint Marks area before my return *vaporetto* ride. My waitress, who came to know me, was happy to practice her English while I practiced my Italian. She taught me how to order my coffee as I liked it: *piu café et poco latte*.

I often took walks to the Rialto area and crossed the bridge to the far side to do some shopping among the local residents. I was well understood by the merchants, and obviously, by shopping here I avoided the pricier costs of items on the other side of the bridge, where tourists abounded. I often purchased sliced prosciutto, bread, and a bottle of wine for my room. I began to feel like a local resident.

On most days, I would walk to the park at the end of the island in the opposite direction from the train station. There, I would sit and study an Italian dictionary that I had bought before leaving home. I would try to learn ten new

Italian words a day from this dictionary. I was happy to improve my knowledge of the language.

Sometime in the summer, the water in the Grand Canal was very low, and as a consequence, a very bad odor permeated Venice. Also, tourists began traveling to Venice, and the streets became quite crowded and difficult to maneuver around the many tourists stopping to gape in all the shop windows. During one of my breakfast jaunts to the Lido in Venice, my waitress had described to me a Lido area away from Venice that was a favored resort of Italian tourists. I decided to leave Venice for *Lido di Jesolo*, which attracted mostly Italian and other European tourists. I checked out of my hotel in Saint Marks Square and wheeled my one large bag up one bridge and down another bridge repeatedly until I reached the *vaporetto* dock. One thing about Venice, traveling with luggage if you are walking any distance can be difficult and cumbersome because there are a multitude of bridges to cross, requiring lifting your bags over steps to cross the myriad of small bridges; rollers on bags did not alleviate this bothersome procedure, as I recall.

Note: I booked my hotels from home from a list of hotels I acquired from the Venice Tourist Board. I decided to book with several different hotels in case I was unhappy with one hotel; I didn't want to get stuck in one hotel that I was unhappy with for my entire stay. I cursed myself for planning my hotel stay in Venice this way, because with every hotel change, and I believe I changed hotels either weekly or biweekly, I found myself wheeling my luggage up and down multiple bridges to reach my new hotel.

Anyway, on to *Lido di Jesolo*. This was an all-day trip from Venice by ferryboat and bus. The Lido was strikingly beautiful, with a long sandy beach, warm soft breezes, and varying hues of blue water as far as the eye can see. I obtained a very comfortable room on a high floor of a hotel overlooking the water. During my stay, one afternoon and evening, I anxiously watched a heavy thunderstorm as water flowed heavily across my balcony. Unlike Venice, this area was less crowded with tourists gaping in shop windows. This was an Italian-speaking resort, and I was pleased that I had learned enough Italian to communicate with people I met or encountered. As a matter of fact, I was quite proud of myself when, one day on the beach, a couple and their brother, all of whom spoke no English, began conversing with me, and through my halting and broken Italian, I conversed with them for two and a half hours before retiring back to my room. I was very proud of myself to have been able to accomplish that challenge.

Touring Venice and Rome with Val and Bobbie

At week's end, I returned to Venice. My sister, Val, and a mutual friend, Bobbie, arrived, and I went to greet them at the train station to accompany them back to my hotel. Val and Bobbie had traveled by train from London and had stopped along the way in Germany and Austria. Bobbie was tall and attractive, with short cropped brown hair, energetic, straightforward, and decisive. She was an avid traveler, had been married to a military officer for about eighteen years, and had lived in various parts of the world. Consequently, she adapted well to new environments. My sister, Val, was feeling poorly. Unfortunately, she had caught a cold while traveling with Bobbie from London to Venice. Normally Val is energetic and ready for any adventure. A cute, petite lady, she is quite attractive, with a short bouffant frosted hairdo, vivacious, and can readily become engaged in animated conversation. She and I are quite opposite that way—I'm the more reserved one. Val is a very giving, thoughtful person who would give you the shirt off her back in a second if needed, without hesitation. On top of her other qualities, she is a very talented seamstress and designer. She designs and sews drapes, wedding gowns, and Batman and other character costumes, but chooses to make things only for the family. Our extended family keeps her quite busy with various sewing projects. I was sorry that Val was under the weather and hoped that she would soon be back to normal.

We all enjoyed a few days together in Venice, taking *vaporetto* rides, shopping the local markets, and visiting the Rialto Bridge and other shopping areas. I took them to the far side of the Rialto Bridge to show them where most of the local people shop. There is one important custom I learned when visiting the outdoor vegetable markets. Unlike in the United States, a customer is not allowed to touch or handle the fruits or vegetables before purchasing. It was a lesson to be learned: if a prospective customer attempted to pick up a tomato or an apple, they got their hand slapped. The custom is to point to your selection and pay for it before handling the product. We enjoyed shopping and visiting the islands of Burano with colorful houses and Murano, where the beautiful Murano glass is blown. We watched the artisans display their talents as they created exquisite handblown colorful glass designs. We enjoyed seeing paintings of various masters as we wandered through museums and churches. We toured palaces, admiring the elegant designs and the exquisite Italian décor and furnishings.

At the end of three days, as planned, we boarded a train from Venice to Rome. The overnight train ride to Rome was quite comfortable, even though we elected not to take sleeping cabins for this trip. We toured Rome and enjoyed sitting in Piazza Navona and many of the other little piazzas, just people-watching or enjoying wine or an ice cream or a bite to eat. Of course, we found our way to the Spanish Steps, the Colosseum, the Vatican, and the Sistine Chapel, and took in most of the major tourist attractions.

On to Barcelona, Spain

I believe we stayed in Rome about five days before boarding another train, this time to Barcelona, Spain, a two-day train ride, where we all disembarked and found a hotel. Barcelona was a beautiful city, with its Gothic architecture and Gaudi's use of natural shapes, color, and imagination displayed in buildings throughout the city, including the beautiful Sagrada Familia Basilica. We visited the Las Ramblas, where we wandered about, looking at the little stands and shops. The Prado Museum was a breathtaking collection of art by such masters as Rubens, Titian, Goya, Rafael, Tintoretto, Velázquez, and so many more. *One could spend hours just soaking in the beauty housed throughout the halls and majestic rooms.* We rode the double-decker bus to tour the city, with all its incredibly detailed and colorful architecture. In contrast to Venice, although there were an abundance of tourists, it didn't compare to the overabundant crowds I experienced in Venice before I left to go to the *Lido di Jesolo* and when I returned to Venice to meet Val and Bobbie. Getting around Barcelona was a little more pleasant because of the more manageable crowds. We made sure to see a bullfight, which was truly an experience. Unlike what we had seen in movies, the bullfighter would try to engage the bull, but before he would kill the bull, he would tease the bull incessantly; and when the bull came near the bullfighter, the bullfighter would pierce the bull with something like a long dart used in a dart game. When the bull was finally exhausted from this taunting and had many of the dart piercings on the back of his neck, I believe it was then that the bullfighter would attempt to kill the bull. We left before what we believed would be the killing of the bull by the bullfighter, because we found this sport and the way it was played to be somewhat nauseating. Thereafter, the excitement and desire to see any further bullfights was quelled. We did, however, enjoy the flamenco dancing at the nightclub floor show that night.

At week's end, it was time for Val and Bobbie to leave Barcelona to continue on to London to catch their return flight home to California.

5

Beautiful Lisbon, A Crossroad Between Moroccan and European Influence

The train ride from Spain to Portugal was very scenic, passing through little towns along the route. I settled into my seat along the window in the six-seat compartment.

In a reflective moment, as the train moved forward from Barcelona, I thought of how far I have come since my initial diagnosis with cancer. I thought back to the turmoil and emotions I experienced during that difficult period -- The gravity of mixed emotions I felt when I realized that I had something in my body that had to be removed; that there was no other alternative; and that, unlike other problems I had experienced, the problems would not go away easily. I recalled that the most difficult thing for me was to accept that I had something inside me that I could not run away from. I had told myself that whereas with most other difficult situations there was a way to possibly set the problem aside for future consideration, ignore the problem, or turn it over to someone else to solve; conversely, in these particular instances, I, and I alone, had to deal with the acceptance of having a harmful *element in my body that had to be dealt with; these were not problems I could turn over to someone else. Just as in accepting death, these were my problems and mine alone. I recalled the trauma of facing my mortality, as well as the fear and anxiety associated with the realization of what was occurring.*

I remembered many moments of just contemplating my situation and wondering if I would ever get beyond the cancer to actually heal and move forward. While reading various books about cancer, I longed to find some more light reading by real cancer survivors, to read about their experiences in overcoming the traumas. I remember thinking then that someone should write a book to fill what appeared to be a void in this type of literature.

I had moved so far beyond that difficult period, and now I was moving forward to enjoy the trips I had dreamed of during my convalescence. I realized that a major part of my moving forward was the time and energy I invested in planning my future and the events and things I would do once I had recovered from my cancer.

* * * * *

Lisbon, Portugal

My plan was to continue on to Lisbon and perhaps go on to Fatima before returning to Venice. I ended up staying about two weeks in Portugal. Moorish architecture was evident throughout Lisbon, and beautiful tile work was displayed on many of the buildings. The *bacalhau* (a dried fish) apparently was a mainstay for many a meal.

The train trip to Lisbon from Barcelona was an overnight trip. I was glad that I was seated in a little seating compartment with six people when I became aware of the conditions developing outside of my little compartment. I had gotten up to go to the toilette and had difficulty opening the compartment door to the narrow hallway. I learned that a young adult traveler lay sleeping against the door that I was trying to slide open. When I finally was able to open the compartment door and attempt to enter the hallway, I saw that almost every inch of the hallways up and down the train was lined with these young travelers sleeping on the floors wherever they could lay their heads. It was very difficult to make my way to the toilette trying not to step on any of the bodies sleeping on the floor. When I finally reached the toilette, opening the door was again almost impossible, as there was a body sleeping on the inside of the little room and I had to physically push and force the door open. I requested the young sleeping adult to exit the toilette so I could use the facility. Returning to my seat was a repeat of the difficulty in reaching the toilette. I vowed to always remember *never travel on a European train in the middle of the summer. This was definitely not an experience I would care to repeat!*

Upon arrival in Lisbon, I retained a hotel room with a bathroom down the hall, as was common in Europe, I learned. *If I could have afforded a first-class hotel with private bathroom, I would have, but I made a choice between staying in far more expensive hotels and shortening the time I would spend on this trip to about six weeks; or being able to spend as much as six months in order to have a true European cultural experience. In the end, I opted for the latter and resolved to accept a private room in a safe neighborhood with shared bathroom as a consequence.* The hotels I selected were all located in very safe areas, were very clean and comfortable except for having to share a bathroom, and offered a European breakfast.

The main problem with traveling alone in countries where you know no one at all was the need to be very aware of your surroundings and the people around you and to always be very careful to protect your finances and traveling documents. Consequently, whenever I left my room to go to the toilette or bathroom, I always wore my passport holder with my passport and important documents on my shoulder and under my armpit. I was extremely careful to protect my passport holder at all times during the six months I traveled around Europe. (By the time I returned home to the United States, it felt at first like I had an indentation where my passport holder had hung around my shoulder under my armpit for six months.)

Having secured my hotel room, I inquired at the front desk where I might find a bookstore. The bookstore was two to three blocks away, and I headed in that direction, along the way checking out the neighborhood, restaurants, and stores where I might find provisions during my stay. I was completely surprised and elated to find one little pocket language book that translated Portuguese to English and vice versa. I was in total disbelief but completely relieved. En route back to the hotel, I stopped to get a bottle of wine, looked at a few menus in restaurants, and picked up some snacks at a little store. I dropped off my purchases in the room and headed for a small neighborhood restaurant, bringing with me my newfound jewel, my little pocket dictionary/language book. During dinner, I perused my book, first to learn important greetings in Portuguese: good morning, good evening, and thank you. Then I went on to learn numbers. I learned how to count to five in Portuguese by the time I finished my dinner. In contrast to Venice, where waiters and waitresses enjoyed practicing their English on me, here in Portugal, few people I came across (other than the hotel desk clerk) knew or spoke English. So when I returned to my hotel room, I continued to study my new language book, learning how to count to thirty. The next morning and subsequent mornings, before I left my room to have breakfast, I studied and eventually learned how to count to one hundred and how to at least order a meal at a restaurant without having to just point to the menu. I learned the basics in shopping—how much?—and now that I had learned my numbers, I could understand the price when I received a response.

After a few days, I was quite comfortable wandering around Lisbon, since at least I now had a very basic understanding of the Portuguese language. The waiters and waitresses warmed to me because they were pleased to have this tourist ordering in their language. One evening at dinner, there was another lady eating alone, and she stopped by my table to converse in English on her way out. She was very pleasant, middle-aged, attractive, and traveling alone as well. We decided to meet for dinner the following night. The second day after I met this lady, we toured around Lisbon together, and I welcomed her companionship. We decided to take a short train trip toward Fatima and ended up in a little fishing village along the way, about fifty miles outside of Lisbon. We each got our hotel rooms for the night, then wandered around the village. It was a really quaint and charming fishing town, but the name now escapes me. The night was warm, a balmy evening with a slight breeze every now and then. There were people fishing along the beach, and families were enjoying the evening just sitting along the beach or around the village square. We ate local fish in a little restaurant and enjoyed a couple of glasses of Vinho Verde, a very special, slightly bubbly Portuguese green wine. The next day, my acquaintance was heading back to Lisbon, and since the distance to Fatima was more than I wanted to travel, I returned to Lisbon as well, returning to the hotel I had been staying in before going to the little fishing village. The following day, my newfound acquaintance left to continue her travels.

A few days later, I decided to take a day train trip to a beach resort south of Lisbon in the Algarve. I was quite taken by the charm of this beach and wished that I had planned to stay for a few days. The little striped beach *tents* (as compared to *beach umbrellas*) were private little tents, enough to fit two beach towels spread out side by side, maybe a little wider, with three canvas sides, a peaked covered roof, and two flaps to close off the front of the tent for privacy. The beach was lined with these little tents. So the idea I surmised was that if you wanted to sunbathe, you could, but you got into the tent to get out of the sun. Unfortunately, I did not have the opportunity to visit the beaches of Cascais and Estoril, closer to Lisbon.

I spent another week of soaking in the local culture in Lisbon, with daily walks around the city, perusing the local markets with displays of *bacalhau*; enjoying the beautiful ceramic tile work displayed in architecture around the city; the Moorish-style citadel of São Jorge Castle sitting majestically atop one of Lisbon's seven hills; the pastel-colored buildings of the Old City; views of the Tagus River; and the warm, friendly feeling of the city. I enjoyed an evening of listening to beautiful *Fado* music. I couldn't understand most of it, but I found *Fado* to exude a sadness and deep thoughtful feelings.

It was time to board the train headed back for Venice. I believe this was about a two-to-three-night train ride.

6

A Very Anxious and Agonizing Return Trip from Portugal to Venice;

Winding Down in Venice

(Post-Cancer #1)

A major earthquake rumbled through San Francisco, creating a major break in the San Francisco Bay Bridge.

My return train trip to Venice was quite a nerve-racking and very anxious trip. In my little shared train compartment, I began noticing pictures on front pages of Italian newspapers being read by other passengers of what appeared to be photos of the Bay Bridge in San Francisco, which had been damaged and split with a large (about a ten-foot) gap, creating two different levels of the bridge. As I looked at various pictures on various front pages, I became totally panicked at what I was afraid might have been the fate of my family back home. I learned that a very sizable earthquake had hit San Francisco and the Bay Area. I got off the train at various points to try to call my family in San Francisco but was unable to get through to anyone. Other passengers were empathetic when they saw how distraught I was at not being able to reach my family. All I could glean from the newspapers was that the earthquake was devastating. I was totally beside myself at not knowing the status of the well-being of my family.

As it turned out, to my good fortune, I had become friendly with an attorney in Milan, whom I had had communication with shortly after arriving in Italy. Before leaving home for this extended trip, when I had seriously thought of the possibility of living in Venice or somewhere in Italy, I researched possible law firms where I might be interested in working, and I sent resumes to various law firms in Milan and elsewhere. I received a response from and had been in contact with Bruno, an attorney in Milan. Bruno was quite distinguished, of medium build, about five feet eight inches tall, with graying temples and a mild and graceful manner. Bruno was entertaining the idea of opening an office in the United States or securing an affiliation with a law firm in the United States. Bruno and I had communicated shortly after I arrived in Italy, and he visited me in Venice a few times. Because he usually had his vehicle, he would take me to areas outside of Venice, and once took me to stay in one of the mansions outside of Venice, securing my own room, which I appreciated.

I felt very fortunate to have someone in Italy whom I could contact in this distressing period. I was able to reach Bruno, and of course, he understood my anguish at not being able to reach my family. I was so thankful to have had at least one person in Italy from whom I could seek comfort and solace. Bruno suggested that I stop and stay in Milan until I could reach my family before continuing on to Venice. After an agonizing period, I was finally able to reach my family and learned that all was well with them, to my great relief. Bruno had been very kind, and we continued communicating long after I returned to the United States. In fact, I later introduced him to the partners in my law firm so he could pursue an affiliation with a US law firm.

The climate was changing around the time I returned to Venice (early September). Temperatures were much cooler to cold, and I found that my summer clothing did not suffice to keep me warm in these temperatures, even by layering my clothing. I began to scour the local markets in search of a warm coat and warmer clothing. I purchased a minimal number of items, as this fall/winter clothing would add substantial weight to my luggage, and moving about could become more difficult.

7

Return to the United States after Six-Month European Experience; Settling Back Home in the United States (Post-Cancer #1)

After my frightful experience of not being able to immediately reach my family following the major San Francisco earthquake, I began to feel a little homesick. I started to rethink whether I would be comfortable living so far away from family on another continent. I flashed back to thoughts of my cancer experience and began to feel the importance of having accessibility to family in times of crisis.

After my return to Venice from Lisbon in the fall, I began to think about and plan to return back home. Throughout Venice, temperatures kept dropping, and many days brought in heavy fog, so it became less enjoyable to wander around the city. I happened to call a very dear friend of mine, Gina, with whom I worked in a law firm in Sacramento, California, prior to going to Venice to live. Gina was a great friend, very petite, with a full head of softly curled, shoulder-length black hair, and very pretty. She was kind and soft-spoken and had a good sense of humor, with a lighthearted and friendly personality. She and I often enjoyed cocktails after work at various cocktail lounges in the area. Before I moved to Venice for six months, Gina suggested that I call her when I was ready to head home. She said, "When you come back from Venice, I probably would have moved back to the East Coast to New Jersey, where most of my family live." She said I should stop off in New York for a few days on my way back to California, to stay with her and her family so I could see and visit the sights of New York.

Around early October, I called Gina from Venice and said I would be returning to California in the next week or so and that I would be making my flight arrangements soon. She was anxious to see me and to hear about the events of the last six months and invited me to stop in New York and stay a little while before continuing on to California. She said her sister, Rita, could pick me up at the John F. Kennedy International Airport in New York City and bring me to Jersey City, New Jersey, to stay with them in their apartment. I was quite reluctant to accept Gina's invitation for her sister, Rita, to pick me up at the airport, since I did not know Rita and had never spoken with nor met or seen any pictures of her. I expressed to Gina my perplexity regarding how we would be able to identify each other. She said she would give me a description of both the vehicle and Rita, and also would give Rita all the specific information regarding my flight. She assured me that Rita would be happy to do this for me and that she wished I would accept her invitation. I felt very assured, accepted and thanked her for the invitation, and proceeded to solidify my flight reservation to New York.

I arrived at the JFK airport in New York sometime in the second week of October. True to her word, Gina had made certain that Rita and I would connect without difficulty. Rita had brought her roommate, Perla, to help her navigate locating and identifying me per Gina's descriptions. Like her sibling, Rita was very petite and attractive, with a short, stylish hairdo. To her credit, Rita was very pleasant, friendly, and gracious. Perla, who was a nurse, had a slightly more authoritative personality but was pleasant and friendly nonetheless. The three of us enjoyed animated conversation during our nearly two-hour ride all the way from JFK airport through Manhattan to their two-bedroom condominium in Jersey City. By the time we arrived, I was completely comfortable with both of them. I realized Rita and Gina, as siblings, shared very similar kind, generous, and pleasant personalities. (Rita and I would later become as good friends as I was with her sister, Gina.) As it turned out, I would stay with them here and make this my home far longer than I had planned. Gina's daughter, Annie, lived in the apartment as well. Annie was an extremely pretty eight-year-old, very animated, friendly, and quite bright. She and I would become very friendly and comfortable with one another, often riding around in Gina's car to run various errands. Annie was eager to learn to cook, and I often had her help me cook meals.

The following day, I had planned to stay home, but my plans would change. The next morning, Gina informed me that she had decided to go to the United Nations (UN) to submit an application for employment. She suggested I go with her so I could get my true introduction into the great city of Manhattan. We would take the PATH train into the city, and I would see the United Nations as well. So since she was putting on a business suit, I decided to put on my most businesslike attire and join her. (For those unfamiliar with the proximity of Jersey City to New York City (Manhattan), it's just a quick PATH train ride through the tunnel to Manhattan from Jersey City, the PATH train probably being the nearest and most direct subway ride and most traveled transportation link between Jersey City and Manhattan. New Jersey is one of the states comprising the tristate area of New York, New Jersey, and Connecticut.) The PATH train ride was about a ten-to-fifteen-minute ride into Manhattan from the Pavona station. From the terminal on Thirty-Fourth Street in Manhattan, we took buses to the United Nations on Forty-Second Street and First Avenue. When Gina took an application to fill out, she handed me one as well and suggested that I, too, submit an application. At first, I was reluctant to do so, but I succumbed to Gina's prodding and completed an application. We spent the better part of our day filling out our applications and being interviewed.

Unfortunately, Gina was overqualified for the position she applied for. I had more options since I had applied for a general office position, and was offered a position in an undersecretary general's office for public information. I was taxed with organizing a severe backlog of incoming correspondence from over 100 missions worldwide. I was to sort, organize and develop files and an efficient filing system that would allow ready retrieval of any correspondence from any of over 100 missions. At the completion of my project, I offered the USG a chronological index of all the correspondence, dates received, subject matter of each, derivative mission, and cross-referenced each correspondence in a separate index of each of the one hundred-plus missions listing all correspondence received from each mission. The USG was satisfied and impressed with my presentation.

8

Homeward Bound (Post-Cancer #1)

Before beginning my job at the United Nations, I returned home to see my mother and siblings in San Francisco, whom I had not seen in six months. My mother had been experiencing ministrokes for about nine months now and needed a twenty-four-hour companion. She was mobile and could walk with assistance but needed the twenty-four-hour care because of the spontaneous ministrokes. Upon returning home and seeing my ailing mother, I began feeling torn between calling the United Nations and advising that I had decided not to accept the position and staying here at home, or returning to New York to begin a new life. I was elated to see my mother above all and, of course, happy to see my siblings. My mother was very disappointed to hear that I would be leaving again soon and wouldn't return for another six months.

At this point, I feel it important to back up and give a more complete reasoning for returning to Venice to live for six months. By now, Tim and I had been married about fifteen years, although we lived separately for eight of the fifteen years. Prior to our separation, we had what I believed to be a beautiful, happy marriage, filled with passion, compassion, kindness, respect, and true love. In retrospect, I now believe that perhaps that description was solely my interpretation of our marriage. Tim and I had dated/courted for seven years prior to our marriage. Tim and I were a handsome couple by all accounts. He was tall, six feet two inches, very handsome and svelte, with dark hair and sideburns, blue eyes, and distinguished-looking, with a nice baritone voice. I was petite, five feet two inches tall, with long, dark, curly hair, brown eyes, and by other accounts, attractive to pretty, with an outgoing personality. Conversely, Tim was dubbed shy and reserved.

Prior to my first trip to Europe with Fran, my husband, Tim, and I had been separated for about eight years, and intermittently we discussed resuming our marriage and combining our households. Invariably, at subsequent moments after each of these conversations, the subject of resuming our marriage would no longer be a high priority in Tim's mind, and we would postpone (again and again) our reunion. During the course of our separation, I often thought of moving away from the Bay Area, since it was slowly becoming apparent to me that my reunion with Tim as husband and wife might not materialize. I thought of moving to Los Angeles (LA) but had not seriously pursued it. Prior to taking my trip to Europe with Fran, I decided to finally put an end to the eight-year indecision by Tim to resume our married life. I advised Tim one night on the telephone that I would be accepting his gift of a two-for-one airline ticket and going to Europe. I asked him again whether he would give me a definite time when we would resume our marriage and move in together. He still could not commit to a time frame. I advised him that this was the last time I would inquire about this subject with him. The next inquiry would have to come from him. I said that when I returned from my sixteen-day tour of Europe, I expected him to communicate to me, soon thereafter, a definite time for us to get back together again; that I would no longer be the one to initiate the subject with him; and that if he was not forthcoming when I returned from Europe, I would be planning my future life accordingly without him. There would be no further initiation or conversation on my part about the subject; I would just begin planning my solo life.

Once I returned from my trip through Europe, Tim didn't mention our possible reconciliation, nor did I broach the subject. About this time I began thinking about returning to Venice. Once I had made the decision to return to Venice for six months and to turn over the responsibility of renting my house to a property manager, I felt this was the perfect opportunity for me to begin a life elsewhere if I decided along that course. I decided that I needed to sever ties with Tim; therefore, I would begin divorce proceedings and advised Tim that I would be serving him divorce papers. He was a bit astonished that I would be doing so. I recalled to him our conversation before I went to Europe, and that since then, he had been silent regarding resuming our marriage. I felt that I had given the situation enough time; it was time to go forth with our individual lives. Tim was not happy hearing this from me, but he said he would cooperate with me and that, in fact, he would attend the hearing with me if I so desired. So prior to my actual move to Venice, I finalized our divorce in order that I would be free to make a decision to move elsewhere. I was so emotionally tied with Tim and could easily revert (as I had been doing for eight years) to waiting for him to make a decision to resume our marriage. I felt the only way I would really be able to get away from him and not be so readily accessible to him would be to physically remove myself from him by distance. In this way, I would hopefully be able to finally sever our ties and emotionally accept the fact that he and I would no longer be husband and wife.

Thus, I was torn in my decision to stay here in San Francisco or the Sacramento area of California or move on to New York (a good distance away) and make a new life. The UN position offered me the opportunity to begin a new life a good distance away from Tim. The sacrifice or drawback was that I would again be away from my ailing mother and my siblings. I felt that I could take this six-month contract position and then decide whether or not to remain in New York. So my decision was to go on back to New York, at least to fulfill the six-month contract. I would end up staying and living in New York from that point to the present (over two decades).

9

Daydreaming—Keep On Truckin'

At various low points in my life, when I am feeling bored or anxious or depressed, rather than succumbing to those emotions or allowing my feelings to accelerate to a point well beyond my comfort zone, I have tried very hard to distract myself from my depression or anxiety by directing my thoughts to more pleasant and happy thoughts or experiences.

My usual direction of thought goes to vacations, sunny beaches, and relaxing moments near a water's edge, drinking a nice tropical cocktail. These thoughts were how I calmed myself during my two-and-a-half to three-hour awake surgery, when I could hear the surgeons' comments as they tried to locate the vein(s) in my head that was or were causing the flare-up of my giant cell arteritis. Although during that procedure I could not feel pain, I could hear the conversations between my surgeons as they used their surgical instruments to move about my head in search of locating the cause of the problem. While listening to them as they redirected their movements several times, I could sense my anxiety level beginning to reach high points. In order to calm my nerves during this long, anxious period, I daydreamed about sunny vacations and enjoying cocktails while sitting on a beach. I reminisced about past family reunion cruises and relived the highlights of those wonderful experiences—the happy emotions I felt as I shared quality time with my siblings and other close friends and relatives.

Therefore, at my lowest points, I daydream. Daydreaming puts me in a form of euphoria, calms my nerves, and allows more pleasant thoughts to enter my psyche and calm my emotions.

I won't say that diverting your attention and thoughts in times of depression or low emotional points is as easy as turning on a light switch—*absolutely not!* Such a practice takes extreme measures on the individual's part to try to lower anxiety while keeping an obstinate focus on overcoming a given situation, depression, or anxiety.

Compare a child growing up in a difficult, adverse childhood environment, who, while living in those adverse circumstances, uses his or her thought processes to develop a plan to remove himself or herself from such an environment. That child may make a decision to eventually be able to progress out of that situation and on to a better life and future, realizing the importance of exercising patience to achieve that goal. This would be an example of the thought analyses, the strength and perseverance that child mustered up in order to succeed in bringing himself or herself out of that environment in order to realize a better, more fruitful, positive future.

I believe most of us are born with the ability to grow and develop thought processes that allow us to make decisions at different points in our lives, like when we reach a fork in the road. At that point, we must make the decision to choose which road to pursue. Such decisions, which we face throughout life, are consequential and often affect the course of our future.

10

New York City, the Big Apple— A Glimpse into a City Like No Other; Settling into a New Life

I think most are familiar with the unbelievable entertainment, theater, museums, and culture available in the great New York City: the wonderful Central Park; the excitement of Times Square; the ferry terminal, where the immense and impressive USS *Intrepid* now lives, and where one can take a ferry tour to the Statue of Liberty; the double-decker buses that tour the downtown and uptown areas of the city and Brooklyn; the World Trade Center monument; the many little outdoor courts and seating areas that have popped up around the city and in Times Square, with vendor food booths available to satisfy your hunger and thirst as you venture around the city; the incredible diversity in food available from around the globe; and the entertaining nature of this great, exciting city.

This chapter includes a few short quips just to give the reader an insight into the city from a resident's viewpoint, a glimpse of living in the City That Never Sleeps.

Settling In

The Upper East Side is a bustling neighborhood replete with little shops offering delicacies and pastries from areas around the globe, such as Italy, Germany, France, Poland, and other parts of Europe. The many delicatessens create an atmosphere one might find in many a European city. Restaurants as well are unique and varied, creating an eating mecca.

After perusing the bulletin board in the cafeteria at the United Nations, I called and settled upon an apartment to share on the Upper East Side of Manhattan on Second Avenue. It was a two-bedroom apartment in a fifth-floor walk-up (no elevators), which I would share with two other ladies. It was very quaint, with a *bathtub in the kitchen*. I procured one bedroom next to the kitchen with slanted floors (meaning not level). It was quite an amusing experience, having a bathtub/shower in the kitchen. I believe I lived there about six to eight months before I moved to a somewhat newer apartment in midtown on Thirty-Fourth Street, within walking distance to my job at a law firm.

Subsequently, I moved back into the original fifth-floor walk-up, another two-bedroom down the hall from the first apartment I had lived in about a year or so earlier. This apartment was a *"railroad apartment,"* meaning all rooms abutted. There were no hallways; you went through one room to enter another room. So, essentially, except for the room in the front, no other room was totally private. This apartment needed about three coats of TLC; the carpets, which were gray before cleaning, were actually a beautiful dark rose color once thoroughly cleaned; the floors were not as slanted; and it also had a bathtub in the kitchen. I turned this apartment into a very quaint and charming one-bedroom apartment with a huge walk-in closet, having converted the entire bedroom in the rear of the apartment into a walk-in closet. I was surprised and amused some years later when reading a magazine article about a very prominent and famous singer, which showed a picture of her apartment on the Upper East Side of Manhattan. I was astounded as I looked at the picture of her apartment, as my apartment was exactly the same layout, with the bathtub in the kitchen and the opening in the wall leading to the living room, just like her apartment.

I loved this Upper East Side neighborhood and was glad to be back. There were restaurants just about on every corner; the renowned and famous Aileen's, which had been around for many years, apparently was installed way back when it was one of the few businesses around. Aileen's was great fun; I could go drinking there and just cross the street to go back home. My new front window looked down on Aileen's. In this area, shopping was so interesting and quaint, with local meat stores and little gourmet shops of many kinds, along with the local supermarkets, bakeries, and pastry shops.

The only thing I didn't like about being back uptown were those god-awful subway rides to work in the hot summer with the unbearable humidity, when I needed a second bath by the time I'd gotten to work!

Midtown Manhattan

I now live on the East Side of Midtown Manhattan, centrally located and close to the United Nations. Consequently, when dignitaries are in town or when our president or other officials are in town, traffic (including walking traffic) is usually hindered or prevented in and around my neighborhood. Forty-Second Street, a main crosstown street in Midtown, is often traversed by motorcades of black SUVs with police escorts. When these motorcades appear, one knows that probably the president is in town visiting. During the General Assembly session of the United Nations in September, security in and around my neighborhood is very tight, and the black SUV motorcades frequently abound along Forty-Second Street, sirens often spewing.

There is an overpass nearby, and in this section of roadway, parking is prohibited during many events throughout the year that require tighter security, such as on the Fourth of July, when people gather in the area to watch the fireworks along the East River. On July 4, in order to be able to drive up the street to my home, photo ID with a neighborhood address is required to gain access. Also during tight security periods, such as the United Nations' General Assembly in September, the mailbox in front of the satellite post office in the building across the street is sealed so that no mail or other items can be inserted in it.

My long-time friend Eric and I are partners in a small business. We have, in the past, had brick-and-mortar stores on the Upper East Side, in the Village in Manhattan, and in Long Island. We complement each other in business. Eric is medium-built and handsome, with dark, curly hair. He is quick-witted and has an uncanny ability to describe people he comes to know in the funniest, lighthearted descriptions. He brings out laughter in people by offering them descriptions and imitations of themselves. Out of the clear blue, he will spout

out a funny phrase that brings laughter or amusement to anyone around. I often am amused and wonder how he comes up with his various quips at such opportune moments.

One time, when Eric and I were returning from having worked our craft market (see chapter 12 for more details on this profession), we had packed all our market equipment and goods into the car, and the car was packed as we headed home. As we turned onto our street from Third Avenue, we came upon a roadblock, with the New York Police Department blocking the road. We were asked for ID, and thankfully, I did have mine, with a local address. However, when the police opened the back doors and found the back of our car packed to the ceiling, with only fabric covering visible, the police officers circled our vehicle with security dogs sniffing around the outside and under the vehicle. This was a bit unnerving, but living in my area, one could expect unexpected security measures to pop up at any time. Anyway, we were allowed to continue on to the next block to go up the hill. Midway up the block, another NYPD car, parked perpendicular to the street, moved over to allow us through so we could finally move up the hill. It was an incredible feeling; at first we felt like criminals; then we felt like dignitaries or important people. The security could be likened to (I would imagine) passing clearance for anyone visiting the president of the United States at the White House.

Movie Filming and Consequences to Residents

Another wonderful aspect of living in my neighborhood (and I say this facetiously) is that it is a popular location for filming movies and TV shows. Parking spaces in and around Manhattan are at a premium, and luckily in my neighborhood, if you can wait patiently for a parked vehicle to exit a space, you can acquire a space for a night or two (currently free, without any fee). (See the next chapter regarding alternate sides parking in NYC.) So if you are lucky enough to secure a space, you cherish that space. Unfortunately, several times during the year, movie and filming companies secure permits to oust parked vehicles from their spaces for usually at least a twenty-four-hour period. Consequently, many times, especially during the spring and summer months, one can see colored flyers posted to poles lining the streets, advising that vehicles must be removed from their parking spaces or be towed. On occasion, these signs are posted just a few hours before the vehicles must be removed, rather than giving at least a full twenty-four-hour notice. For tourists or visitors, it can be entertaining to watch the filming of a movie, but for a resident who has been ousted from a coveted parking space, this becomes a chaotic circumstance in which one must find a temporary location for a vehicle for the twenty-four-hour period, or longer, that filming is taking place. To my knowledge, in all the years I have lived here, the filming companies have never compensated residents for this inconvenience.

This instance of being ousted from a coveted parking space, especially when not given ample notice, is an instance where I have to exercise my self-training of mental probing in order to quell my anxiety and try to find a positive element in the situation. It's tough to think positively under this circumstance; the only positive thought I can come up with is the fact that, apart from the days when I must move my vehicle to allow for the filming of a movie, most other days I do have the ability, with patience, to acquire a "free" parking space for possibly two days at a time.

Summer in the City

If you visit New York, take public transportation. Particularly in the summer, it's best if you do not drive a vehicle in the city. During the summer, the city is replete with street fairs along many of the avenues, resulting in many main north/south (some east/west) streets being blocked to traffic.

Unfortunately, although one can usually learn in advance of street closures for the main parades, there is usually no forewarning or posting anywhere I'm aware of that posts the closing of streets for the myriad of street fairs that take place during the spring, summer, and fall months. Consequently, if you're driving in the city, be prepared to be diverted from your route because several blocks have been barricaded for a street fair. And since almost every street in Manhattan is a one-way street, when you get diverted, you must go several blocks out of your way (usually long blocks) before turning back to continue. This becomes most frustrating when, for instance, a northbound avenue is blocked by a street fair, and then the next available northbound avenue is also blocked for another street fair. One can spend hours circulating the city to get to a location.

Once, there was either a bike race or a marathon, which route went from Staten Island, then north through Manhattan along Sixth Avenue to Central

Park, blocking some north/south streets and many crosstown streets along the way. On this particular day, we needed to get to work in the Village on the west side of downtown Manhattan, traveling from the east side of midtown Manhattan. Unfortunately, we had not journeyed out early enough. We started on our usual route down Second Avenue, then tried to cross over to the west side on about Twenty-Ninth Street, but were blocked on Fifth Avenue from going west. We continued all the way down to Houston and got to within four blocks of our destination but were blocked from crossing Sixth Avenue. We turned back and went downtown along the east side all the way to Battery Park to try to go across to the west side but were blocked by police officers (the Brass), who advised us that we had to go all the way back uptown on the east side to about One-Hundredth street, cross over to the west side, then drive back downtown to Third Street to our ultimate destination.

Through this lesson, I learned to pay attention on Friday nights to the events around the city on Saturday morning, knowing that we must get to our market location on those Saturdays by a quarter to six or earlier even though the market does not open until nine o'clock and setup doesn't begin until around seven thirty or eight.

11

New York City Parking Rules: Alternate Sides Cleaning

*I*analogize waiting for a New York City residential parking space to waiting for a jackpot to hit. You sit and wait and watch a street lined with parked cars on both sides. All of a sudden, you hear a click, click or see a taillight blink and light up, and you race to get in place for that car to move. You've hit the jackpot! The parked car exits and frees up the space, and "Bingo," you're in; just as a jackpot's bells ring, the machine spills its coins, and the gambler scoops up his winnings! (How long did it take this time—thirty minutes, one hour, two hours, or more?)

New York City is really unique in how it handles parking spaces and street cleaning on certain days. At the end of the day, one really has to appreciate the humor in the ridiculousness and comical manner in which street cleaning is accomplished in this city.

There are so many parking signs prohibiting parking. The signs most affecting resident parking are the "alternate sides cleaning" parking rules. Here are some typical restrictive signs:

No Parking	8:30–10:00 a.m. Monday & Thursday
No Parking	8:30–10:00 a.m. Tuesday & Friday
No Parking	10:00–11:30 a.m. Monday & Thursday
No Parking	10:00–11:30 a.m. Tuesday & Friday
No Parking	11:30 a.m.–1:00 p.m. Monday & Thursday
No Parking	11:30 a.m.–1:00 p.m. Tuesday & Friday

And there are many more variations of the above.

New York City must have the largest collection of prohibitive parking signs of any city in the world. And, to boot, I have personally been caught in a dilemma of trying to figure out which signs to follow within the same block. I once attempted to park my car overnight around the corner from me on a very busy main avenue. After reading three prohibitive parking signs on one end of the block, then verifying and finding two different and somewhat conflicting prohibitive parking signs at the other end of the same block, I opted to find parking elsewhere. It's a good thing I checked the signs at both ends of the block before parking there, or I might have found my car had been towed when I returned the next morning.

Anyway, returning to the alternate sides cleaning rules, they function slightly differently block to block, so one must determine which procedure to follow by checking the posted signs within not only a particular block but also which side of the block because signs are typically different on opposite sides of a particular block. Also, each block handles moving their vehicles when the street sweeper appears according to that block's own unique procedure, which can be different from block to block.

So on your particular cleaning day, for instance, if you are parked in a "No Parking 10:00–11:30 a.m." section, you must be seated in your car by ten o'clock and remain within your vehicle until eleven thirty. Within my neighborhood, we sit and wait until we see the street sweeper. Now, the following steps are very important, and you must be extremely alert and quick so as not to lose your space to an encroaching driver, who will try to steal your parking space. Our street sweeper usually arrives about forty-five minutes past the hour. So, around that time, you should be looking in your side-view mirror for the approaching street sweeper. When you see the street sweeper vehicle at the end of the block, you pull out and park parallel to the car parked on the opposite side of the street, in order to allow space for the street sweeper to glide along the curb where your car had been parked. As soon as the street sweeper passes your vehicle, you must immediately pull back into your original parking space. This becomes very tricky, because you must pull in headfirst, then forward, and then back into your space, all the while watching the vehicles in front of you and behind you doing the same thing while cars are passing through the neighborhood, and simultaneously trying to avoid a collision, while also making sure that no parking space thief takes your space. This is a very nerve-racking and harrowing procedure, which must be mastered. I have now had about three years of experience doing this; therefore I've become a little more comfortable with the procedure. Ideally, and what I used to do when I started doing this, was to pull out almost perpendicular to the parking space I just left; then I would just back into the space I vacated after the street sweeper passed, which to me is far more efficient; however, more veteran parkers prefer that it be done as I explained at first.

Although this procedure can be very stressful, one can't help but find humor in it, as it really is, in my opinion, a rather quirky procedure. However, I must say, it does allow residents to park on the city streets without paying the exorbitant parking fees of garages. The most frustrating part is first securing a parking space. Oftentimes getting a parking spot in the first place requires waiting in your car for an hour or longer until someone leaves a spot. My average waiting time is about one to one and a half hours, but I have waited multiple hours for a parking space to become available.

One morning, as I was walking back to our craft market on Seventh Avenue, I was crossing a side street when I saw cars pulling out of their parking spaces in succession and parallel parking alongside the cars on the opposite side of the street. At first, as I watched, I thought it rather peculiar, but then I remembered it must have been alternate sides cleaning day. I watched, and as the street sweeper passed, the drivers began re-parking their vehicles, and the street became replete with vehicles moving in all different directions, as other passing vehicles tried to maneuver between the reparking vehicles. I observed with apprehension several near misses of cars colliding with one another. I laughed to myself in amusement, as it was quite a funny happenstance to watch if one didn't know what was happening. It truly is a New York phenomenon, and one has to find amusement in watching these cars as they then fight to get back into their parking spaces—very expertly, I might add, as rarely does an accident happen. New Yorkers are quite adept in adhering to this procedure, but it really is quite amusing to watch it taking place. I know in my area, there are many retirees, and some often stop in amusement to watch this occur, as it happens four times every week. They usually walk away chuckling and shaking their heads.

12

A Look into the Life of a New York City Market Vendor

There are hundreds, perhaps thousands, of activities visible and evident as one meanders around New York City at any given time of the year. Particularly during the warm summer months, outdoor activities abound—bike races, marathons, triathlons, parades, celebrations of various cultural fairs, shopping, and street or craft fairs—an unbelievable expanse of activities to electrify the psyche and keep the adrenaline of any visitor peaked and alive. Thus, New York, dubbed the City That Never Sleeps, lives up to its calling. The electrifying energy of this great city can be felt even before one actually steps foot onto the streets of Manhattan.

My part in that activity is my involvement in the outdoor craft fairs nine months out of the year, from April through December, when this outdoor activity is more tolerable and quite pleasant on days when the temperatures do not reach the intolerable extremes of freezing or below in winter or 95–110 in the summer. But there are other drawbacks and difficulties of doing business and participating in the outdoor craft/market fairs. First of all, year-round during any day at any time, winds may become fierce, and a thunderstorm or two may appear in the middle of the day, requiring vendors to scramble to cover their products to protect them from damage and grab their market tents and/or umbrellas so as not to succumb to the wind and rain.

But for the most part, this occupation still remains, for most vendors, most enjoyable, albeit not as profitable in today's economy as the public may believe, but rather, to my chagrin, quite to the contrary. Most enjoy working in the outdoors as well as the interaction with the public. I believe that vendors are very quick-thinking and some of the most creative and innovative creatures. A case in point: a vendor who signs up for a new market must analyze the space assigned and quickly mentally create and design an appealing display to attract customers to his or her booth—all while making sure that props, display items, and tents or umbrellas are secured in the event of strong winds or an outburst of thunderstorms or rain. Usually the vendor is given about an hour or so to set up the booth before prospective customers begin appearing. Markets usually begin at ten in the morning and end about six in the evening. Upon closing, the vendors must usually allow a little more time than setup in order to repack their vehicle to fit all fixtures and so on. Most vendors' vehicles are packed quite precisely in order to fit all their wares.

I will now take you with me to share a day in my life as a vendor. I usually begin my day by leaving home at about five thirty in order to secure a parking space near my booth by six in the morning. Most of the fairs where I vend are church markets, which are set up along the outside walls and sidewalks of a church. My most regular market is downtown in the Village, which is where I will vend today. This particular day was quite eventful and one of my most memorable worst days of working the markets. On this nice late-summer day, I did my regular setup to display my designer fashion hats and jewelry. My setup usually takes me about one and a half hours.

The day was proceeding normally, often a slow start and with spurts of customers beginning in early afternoon. Along about three thirty or four o'clock, I began to sense that rain might be approaching. I usually am pretty adept at studying the cloud movements, wind, and temperature variations during the day when I begin to sense ominous weather approaching. Most of the other vendors usually pay attention when they see me begin to pack in the middle of the day. On this day, by the time I noticed that temperatures were cooling rather quickly and that I should pay attention, the rain was about to hit. I was able to quickly grab about six armloads of merchandise and throw them into the car to keep them from getting wet. Both I and my neighbor, Lily, were caught off guard. All of a sudden, it started to rain, not too heavily at first, and both Lily and I were able to put plastic tarp over most of our goods before the rain quickly accelerated to a heavy, windy rain as we desperately tried to save our booths and merchandise. The rain and wind did not let up, and for the next ten to fifteen minutes, Lily and I frantically tried to cover our booths while battling the wind and rain. Finally, in desperation, she and I just looked at each other, stopped and shrugged our shoulders, and dropped our arms to our sides as the rain continued to pound. At that point, we both just laughed, figured the attempt was futile, then threw up our arms and let the rain and wind come down as it wished. We had done the best to save our booths; then we began to laugh hysterically, turned our faces up to the rain, and just took a bath in the rain. *Finally, my unfulfilled childhood desires of wanting to go outside and play in the rain were being fulfilled, as Lily and I hooked arms and danced in the rain.* It continued to rain for about another twenty minutes or so. By the time it stopped, everything was soaked, and Lily and I just stood there, exhausted, with our hair and clothes dripping as if we had just stepped out of a shower (which, in fact, we had). I guess both Lily and I had the most difficult setups, since by now all the other vendors had managed to pack up and leave. I tried to salvage what I could; thank God I was able to throw my hats into the car before the heavy rain started. I began packing up the car as quickly as I could, throwing wet tablecloths, tables, and so on in the car, fearful that another rainstorm would start. After I got the car packed, I stood against the church wall for about a half hour to let the clothes on my body dry a little, since I was totally soaked.

  After about twenty-five minutes, I got into the car to go to the storage room to drop off my goods. When I turned the key in the engine, nothing happened. I tried again, and one more time. *I just couldn't believe it! It never occurred to me that something else could go wrong after the horrible experience I had just endured.* Well, after sitting in my wet clothes and soaking up my dilemma (no pun intended), I thanked my stars that I had AAA road service. I called AAA and was told I probably had to wait about an hour for a tow truck to either start my engine or tow my vehicle to a garage for repair. Thank God, the tow truck finally came after about an hour, and the AAA mechanic was able to jump-start my car. When I was sitting in the car this morning, I played the radio for about forty-five minutes while waiting to set up my booth. Apparently, I should have then restarted the engine to let it run a few minutes before letting it sit for the day—or so the mechanic advised me. Finally, after letting the engine run for a few minutes, I headed to the storage room to store my car contents. I crossed my fingers that my car would start again. Thank God, it did. Now to go home and wait for a parking space to open up. Hopefully, I will get a space soon, so I can get out of my wet clothes, shower, and bundle up for the night.

This was, and still is, the worst day in my life as a New York City vendor!

13

An Unbelievably Stupid Move

One Saturday evening after a long day at the market, we got everything packed into the car and the goods covered with black fabric so as to shield the items from view.

I got into the car and began my trek through the crazy traffic in Manhattan. I took a left onto Carmine after an NYPD vehicle passed, and a taxi driver got in behind the police car. The three vehicles (NYPD, taxi, and I) were stopped at a red light waiting to make a left turn onto Sixth Avenue. The police car had stopped to allow pedestrians to cross. All of a sudden, the taxi driver veered right to go around the police car to make an improper left turn from the second lane. I just automatically followed the taxi driver and went around the NYPD vehicle to make a left as well. As I was completing my turn, I said to myself out loud, "Oh my God—what have you done? Did you just bypass a cop who was sitting there letting pedestrians cross? Holy mother of ____, you just circumvented a cop sitting at a light waiting for passengers to cross. Oh, how stupid, stupid, stupid. You went around a cop to make an illegal left turn. Oh my God!"

By the way, in New York City, it is a rather common driving habit for vehicles to make a left from the second lane, and conversely, make a right from the second lane over—these are illegal turns but nonetheless are common practices. However, the street from which I turned was a one-lane street, not a multilane street, so the taxi and I squeezed around the cop to make that *illegal turn*—and did you get that?—*we went around the cop!* My only excuse for such a stupid move was that I was thoroughly exhausted, and although I could drive safely, apparently my senses were not too acute.

Well, as I completed my turn, I waited for that red blinking light flashing on the police car that completed the turn directly behind me. Sure enough, half a block down, there was the flashing, blinking red light atop the NYPD car.

The officer later told me that when the taxi went around him, he said to his partner, *"Did you see that?"* He was going to go after the taxi, but then all of a sudden, I came around right behind the taxi. He was in disbelief. So, of course, the officer asked for my driver's license, and as I pulled out my driver's license, I apologized sincerely, explaining that I had made a senseless move. I had just completed a long day at my outdoor market at the church behind us and was really tired and anxious to get home. He asked me to unlock the back door behind me, but the lock on my side didn't work for that door. I apologized and said it was an old car and the locks didn't work in the normal fashion, so I leaned across to the front passenger lock to unlock the door behind me. Then the other officer asked me to open the right back door, and I had to repeat the opposite procedure of unlocking the right back door with the lock on my door on the left side. After the officers peeked in through the open doors, the officer beside me very nicely handed me my license and said he was just going to give me a warning and to be careful driving. "There are a lot of pedestrians out there." (Phew!)

I thanked the officer, and we bade each other a pleasant evening.

I fully expected to get a big ticket, and I did deserve it, but I guess the officer took pity on me when I explained that I had worked a long day at an outdoor market, had a car loaded to the top, and was driving a rather old, somewhat inferior car. He was a very kind officer. But I still can't believe that stupid move!

***THE FOLLOWING FOUR CHAPTERS ARE
UNRELATED, AMUSING, LIGHTHEARTED STORIES
OF PRE- AND POST-CANCER EVENTS***

14

Early Cruising with "Bella"

I'd like to share one of my early cruising experiences, an experience that helped to develop my love of cruising.

About a year after my first cancer, I was working in a law firm in San Francisco and had decided I wanted to take another cruise (this would, I believe, have been my fourth cruise). This time, rather than booking a "guaranteed share" cruise, I decided to take the cruise with a fellow coworker in my law firm, a person I did not know but knew of. "Bella" (as later dubbed by her Italian male friend on the cruise) had heard through the grapevine that I would be taking a cruise and might be open to having a cruise mate. So she approached me, and we talked about it. Bella, an attractive, petite lady with short blonde hair was vivacious, spirited, and spunky. She apparently had a reputation in the law firm of being disagreeable at times. This, however, had no bearing on my final decision, since my main focus was to find a cruise mate who was honest and trustworthy and would basically just share cabin accommodations in order to minimize the cost of the cruise fare. I was not necessarily interested in finding a traveling companion, as I was perfectly comfortable traveling alone. I thought Bella would be a good fit for a cruise mate.

I decided to invite Bella on my cruise. This turned out to be one of my most life-altering decisions, as Bella and I have become the closest of friends for decades now.

As a matter of fact, years later when I learned that my cancer had returned after seven years, Bella was very supportive; she was a good consoler and source of comfort during that difficult period. I had no health insurance at the time, and she was instrumental in helping me check resources and facilities where I might be able to get assistance. Bella was very knowledgeable regarding health matters and was a strong, supportive force in helping me think through and learn to accept and deal with this recurrence of cancer. Over ensuing years, she and I have been good for each other in bouncing around thoughts and just commiserating about life and current social and political events.

Anyway, Bella and I selected a cruise to the Caribbean, visiting and touring the Virgin Islands of Saint Thomas and Saint Croix, with beautiful sun-filled sandy beaches and hues of blue water softly lapping against the shores, and also visited Cozumel with its Mayan ruins. The cruise culminated on a private island, where we enjoyed a barbecue and live music on the beach hosted by the cruise line.

During our cruise, Bella became quite acquainted with an Italian engineer working on the ship. So a romance was sparked.

While we were on this initial cruise together, Bella would meet her beau after he was off duty, around eleven o'clock at night. Meanwhile, Bella and I would have a great time wandering the ship partaking in various functions but not before having our morning "room service" cappuccinos. At night, we'd frequent the disco and sit, observe, and laugh about the various passengers and their goings-on. We were quite entertained and amused by watching their behavior and expressions. Bella was a great companion, and she found humor in just observing people. She was prone to spontaneous, infectious laughter that one couldn't help but laugh with her.

Other times during the day, we went our separate ways. I enjoyed sunbathing, while Bella took various shore excursions. Once, in Saint Croix, I wandered through local shops looking for some reggae music to buy. I didn't realize that if you wanted reggae, you'd go to Trinidad or somewhere similar. Anyway, I really didn't find much reggae to my liking.

Bella and I had a great time. We became friendly with the bartender in the disco where Bella and I ended up at nights. After about eleven o'clock, Bella and I would go our own ways.

On the last night of this cruise, Bella got totally sloshed. She was with her beau but had to race to our room during their date, as it turned out, to get sick and throw up in our bathroom. Her beau (Mario) apparently didn't understand Bella's urgency to get to our room, so he started to follow her as she ran to the toilet, and his eyes bugged out with the realization when she started to throw up into the toilet. In her haste to get to the toilet with Mario in the way, he stepped on her baby toe, and we think her toe broke. Needless to say, Bella was feeling no pain and didn't realize her toe had been damaged until the next morning when we were waiting in a large lounge to disembark the ship from this cruise. Bella was afraid she would lose contact with Mario, but he found her before we disembarked, and they exchanged contact information.

Once off the ship, Bella and I proceeded to our hotel in Miami. I was interested in nothing but sleep and informed Bella of this. She continued to return to the room several times to ask me to join her in a meal. I refused each time, to her astonishment.

I guess by the next day, we did go eat and resumed our cocktails. We chatted quite a bit, and I got to know Bella and her background; I found her to be quite a compassionate person. I was glad we had cruised together and were becoming friends.

Mario did contact Bella after the cruise, and they communicated frequently. Their romance began to bloom. She and her beau would write back and forth, with him struggling to communicate in English and Bella improving her knowledge of the Italian language. Mario and Bella were becoming more fluent in each other's language. Bella would share some of the cute letters Mario would write, and their romance flourished. This frequent communication resulted in Bella's beau bringing her back on the ship to be with him for a week, all expenses paid. Bella was so excited.

Over the next several years, Mario brought Bella back for weeklong cruises about twelve times, always all expenses paid. What a whirlwind romance that was. Unfortunately, because of some miscommunication between them, that romance ended abruptly, with Mario citing *karma* as an end to their romance.

Anyway, as a result of that cruise, Bella and I have continued our friendship for more than two decades.

15

Almost Meeting Elvis

Years ago, when Elvis Presley had a concert in Lake Tahoe, California, I was working in a law firm in San Francisco. Several of us legal secretaries were avid Elvis fans, and we were all so excited at his playing so close to San Francisco (only about four hours away). The hardship was securing tickets to the show, as it was nearly impossible to get through on the telephone line to secure reservations. While we worked, each of us secretaries/fans took turns dialing and redialing and staying on hold for long periods of time, attempting to get reservations for the show. This continued for two days until the tickets were sold out without any of us securing reservations.

We were persistent, however, and decided to make our arrangements to go to Tahoe anyway and stand in the waiting line on the day of the show to hopefully purchase last-minute tickets. We reserved a cabin not far from the casino where Elvis was playing. My memory is a little sketchy, but I believe we had about six of us Elvis fans sharing this cabin. While all the arrangements were going on, one of the secretaries had a brilliant idea to prepare and send to Elvis at his hotel a comical (bogus) legal document in complete legal pleading format naming us as Fans of Elvis (plaintiffs) and Elvis (as defendant), requiring him to appear at our cabin and sing a special performance for us. The summons and complaint were quite well prepared, and we were all certain, from hearing about Elvis's personality and his likely amusement with such a summons, that he would in fact make a personal appearance at our cabin as requested. We were all so excited as we planned our trip to Tahoe.

On the Saturday we arrived in Tahoe, we all immediately went to Harrah's Club, where Elvis was appearing, and stood in the long waiting line to hopefully obtain reservations for the night's show. After a long wait, we finally secured our reservations, and we were just ecstatic that we would be able to see the show. En route back to the cabin, we stopped and bought a couple of bottles of champagne to celebrate our good fortune. We all sat around enjoying our champagne, watching the driveway for Elvis's entourage to appear for our special summoned appearance. Well, we all got very happy, and all ended up falling asleep. Needless to say, there was no Elvis appearance at our cabin. As I recall, we had reservations for the 6:00 p.m. show, and I think it was I who woke up at 5:55 p.m., absolutely horrified at the prospect that after all we went through, we would miss our long-awaited show! We had all been so thrilled at finally getting our reservations this morning that we celebrated ridiculously excessively (and stupidly) and as a consequence would miss the performance entirely. I jumped up and awakened the others with the horror of our situation. Collectively, we couldn't believe our stupidity and bad luck. We commiserated, knowing that we had lost our 6:00 p.m. reservation. The drive alone from our cabin to the casino was about ten to fifteen minutes, and we still would have to park our vehicle and get to the show. Also, I believe latecomers were not to be seated.

Well, after commiserating at our horrible misfortune, one of my mates, who was a little more mature and experienced than most of us, informed the others that she might have a solution to getting us into the later show at 9:00 p.m. She said that when she had gone on dates to dinner clubs, nightclubs, and floor shows, she noticed her date would give the maître d' a hefty tip prior to seating, and they always received prime seating. This mate (we'll dub her "Lindy") said that we should all get dressed and go stand in the guest seating line, and when we reached the maître d', she would be the one to approach him. What she did was show him our reservations for the 6:00 p.m. show and explain our situation while handing him a twenty-dollar bill. Before we knew it, we were all being escorted to the second or third row from the stage. *We were so absolutely thrilled* and jumping for joy that Lindy could pull this off and thanked her profusely. Needless to say, this was one of the best Elvis performances I have ever seen, and I have seen many in subsequent years. He was masterful, with an incredibly mesmerizing voice. Every song he sang sent us to heaven. When he sang "Help Me," one could hear a pin drop in the audience. The entire audience was hushed and mesmerized. At the last note of the song, a man sitting near us expressed his amazement at Elvis's incredible voice and performance. He indicated he had never ever witnessed such a mesmerizing performance. I, and all of us, of course, shared in his sentiments. *This was definitely a night to remember!*

The next morning, as we sat eating breakfast while reliving our experiences of the day before, all eyes were on the driveway, still hoping and anticipating that Elvis and his entourage would be driving up the driveway to our cabin. We just knew that he would have been quite amused with our summons for him to come and sing to us in our cabin and would likely humor us by complying with our request. However, disappointingly, he never appeared as we had hoped.

About a week after our weekend in Tahoe for Elvis's performance there, the envelope that was addressed and mailed to Elvis at Harrah's in Tahoe prior to his show was returned to our office marked "Refused —EP." Unfortunately, the secretary who prepared and mailed the document had written on the bottom left-hand corner of the envelope "LEGAL DOCUMENT ENCLOSED." We surmised that because Elvis and his team probably thought this might have been a paternity suit or something similar, he never even opened the letter. Can you believe our incredible (bad) luck? But we did have the memory of a *fantastic Elvis weekend*. (I don't know who ended up with the returned "refused" document. I looked for it once years later; unfortunately, I have lost contact with all my cohorts on that trip.)

Note: My memory is a little sketchy on the details of this long-ago event; however, my recollection as depicted here is very close, if not as things actually transpired.

16

Third Time Is Not a Charm!

One day about a year after my brother Ted died, my sister-in-law and I wanted to go to Mass at Saint John's. We had not planned to attend Mass at this time, but at 9:15 a.m., we decided to try to attend the 10:00 a.m. Mass. We both scurried to get dressed and left the house a little late, at 9:52 a.m. When we arrived at the church, we were unable to find any parking without having to park about two blocks away, which would make us considerably late for Mass. We decided to run an errand or two and wait for the next Mass, at 11:00 a.m.

We took a quick run to the drugstore, about five minutes away, so we could get some photos copied from my camera card. Well, this entailed a long wait since we needed assistance with the printer/copier and the clerk was busy with another customer. Consequently, we were delayed for the 11:00 a.m. Mass and arrived there about 11:00, but again we could not readily find a parking space. Oh well, just our luck. So we'd try again.

We opted for a third attempt to attend Mass but wanted to go to a drugstore about a ten to twelve minutes' drive away. We arrived at the drugstore, and I purchased my items quickly. We got about three blocks away from the church at 11:40 a.m. and were passing a dollar store. We decided to stop in the store for about five minutes since we would have to wait until the parishioners at the church vacated their parking spots. At 11:50 a.m., we headed to the church and arrived as people were leaving the church and exiting the parking area. We secured a very handy space right in front of the church's main steps. My sister-in-law ran ahead while I parked the car. I locked my car and began ascending the church steps when she met me at the top with an agonized, disappointed face and blurted, "This is a Spanish-speaking Mass—no English," and we both groaned. We couldn't believe our luck! We had to laugh as we both realized and said to each other, "No wonder we could find a parking space so easily!"

We got in the car and just looked at each other with quizzical, disappointed faces, and when we spoke, we agreed that going to Mass today was not to be. We both figured the third time was not a charm and headed home!

17

A Perplexing, Extraordinary Experience

Around February 2017, my sister, Val, and I, along with a friend, Art, went to the San Francisco International Airport to pick up my sister-in-law, who was returning from a family emergency trip abroad.

Before returning from the airport, we all decided to go have lunch and were riding on Highway 280 toward Serraville to find a Chinese seafood buffet restaurant, at which Val and I had once enjoyed a handsome buffet.

I was driving, Val was in the front passenger seat, and the other two passengers were in the back seat.

As I was driving, going at a pretty fast speed, as was my customary driving habit, I began to have a very unusual sensation—one of my mind being pulled away from my body—and simultaneously there was a thin white veil, something like a very, very thin layer of white cotton that covered the entire scenery ahead, above, and all around me. Through this white veil, I could see the highway ahead of me and the trees, shrubbery, hillsides, and surrounding communities around us and in the distance, all behind the white-cotton, filmy veil. The other three passengers in the vehicle were engulfed in very loud, animated discussions, with all three talking at once and over one another.

As I was experiencing this unusual sensation of my mind pulling away from my body, I began to sense an impending untoward event about to happen, and I became acutely aware that the wheel and the vehicle were in my control, and that if an untoward event were to happen, there were three other lives that would be affected.

I decided to give a warning to my passengers of impending doom and yelled out loud in order to be heard above their loud conversations: "Heads up, everybody," as I began to reduce my speed to pull off to the side of the road. Even so, the only one heeding my warning was my sister, who asked, "What's happening?" Immediately upon her question, everything returned to normal—the white thin veil left the scenery, and I returned to a sense of normalcy, both in mind and body. As such, I was able to respond to my sister's query, stammering as I uttered, "Uh, oh, nothing, I guess; it's all right," and I continued to drive, quite shaken by the experience.

18
Life Goes On Beyond Bumps and Grinds

*I*llnesses of every kind and in varying degrees of severity take an emotional and physical toll on the affected individual and his or her loved ones. Unfortunately, this element of life and survival is an inevitable experience for most people in our earthly lifetimes. How individuals cope with and survive the pain and agony associated with illness are often dependent upon the subject's ability to grasp the situation and to allow an element of acceptance. The success of coping with illness can be aided by deep introspection, along with faith, love, understanding, and support of loved ones. Perhaps then the affected individual may see a way forward beyond the illness.

I have been aided in coping with my illnesses by trying to look at life and its obstacles in as favorable a lens as I am able to. I strive to find humor in adverse circumstances when and if possible. Although I am not always successful, this attitude helps me to develop a more positive outlook on life.

19

The Battle of Excruciating Effects of Rheumatoid Arthritis (RA)

The effects of rheumatoid arthritis can be likened to a car without lubrication for its moving parts.

If you're unfamiliar with rheumatoid arthritis, it can be (I guess depending upon the severity) very debilitating. I first felt the effects of rheumatoid arthritis while on one of our family reunion cruises in 2004. Midway through the cruise, I began having difficulty walking because of excruciating pain in my joints from the waist down when walking. I had to resort to hanging onto rails and banisters in stairwells and hallways to prop myself up while trying to walk. (Unlike osteoarthritis, which I believe is arthritis pain in localized areas, RA is a condition of a compromised immune system affecting many areas and joints of the body. At least, that's my layman's definition.) Thankfully, these symptoms appeared toward the latter part of the cruise. I had strongly considered requesting the use of a wheelchair for the balance of the cruise.

Once home, I went to see my doctor, who took many blood tests to rule out gout and diabetes, among other diseases. While awaiting results of the tests, she would not prescribe any pain medication or medication to alleviate discomfort without first diagnosing my ailment. I resorted to taking Tylenol in lieu of prescription medication. This was not very helpful in relieving pain in my joints when attempting to administer the functions in the list below. Finally, she diagnosed me with rheumatoid arthritis and referred me to an appropriate specialist. My RA doctor also would not prescribe a pain-relieving medication without completing a series of tests. Meanwhile, as you can see from the following list of adverse difficulties with RA, without medication to relieve the inflammation caused by RA, one can lie like a board, unable to move or function without excruciating pain.

My dear friend Bella suggested that I try noni juice, which is juice from the noni fruit grown in Tahiti. In my desperation of waiting for test results before getting pain-relieving medication, I decided to try a specific noni juice that Bella highly suggested. I opted for expedited delivery and began with quadrupling the dosage. To my relief, the inflammation began subsiding, and within a few days, I was able to walk all around the city, thirty to forty-five blocks at a time, to my various appointments and errands. By the time my RA doctor was ready to prescribe medication for me, I resisted, but he informed me that I had an increasingly debilitating condition that would advance over time and that I needed to take the injections he was prescribing as a preventative measure to keep my condition from deteriorating further. I took him at his word and took the prescription for weekly injections, which I take to this day.

In the list below are just some of the difficulties faced by RA patients when not able to take proper medication; most of the following movements bring pain in arm and finger joints. Pain can also extend to other joints.

1. Pushing the spray knob on the hair spray can

2. Unscrewing the cap on an orange juice carton

3. Extreme pain when attempting to brush teeth, because of arm and joint movements

4. Pulling the tab on a soda can, due to pain in the finger joints

5. Pulling off foil on a small yogurt container (teeth can be used as an alternative to fingers to pull)

6. Removing caps on various medicine containers
7. Pushing a button to start a microwave
8. Holding a fork
9. Slicing an apple
10. Slicing a piece of ham
11. Holding a pen and writing
12. Tearing off a candy wrapper
13. Turning a key in a lock
14. Pulling on socks
15. Putting on closed-heel shoes, even with a shoehorn
16. Pulling a sheet across the body
17. Pulling files out of a filing cabinet

I analogize the severe effects of rheumatoid arthritis to a car without oil for the moving parts. Without the oil, the parts won't move. Conversely, without proper medication to counter the attack on the immune system, the joints in the body are immovable independently without excruciating pain.

20

Sharing Thoughts from My Introspection

I have heard and read from various sources that people who have confronted their mortality develop a change in their attitude toward life in general, attributing less importance to the little nuisances that cross all our paths in daily life. As a result, they develop a more carefree, less urgent sense about hindrances in life than does a person who has not had the experience of confronting his or her mortality. I believe this to be true, particularly in my experience. Since I first was diagnosed with cancer and having experienced the fear and the turmoil of emotions associated with learning of such a life-threatening diagnosis, I have learned to face a given situation and quickly assess the circumstances surrounding an event. I determine whether the circumstance at hand truly is a very grave and serious situation warranting the attention, devotion of energy, and emotions accompanying such grave situations, as opposed to what in my mind can be quickly set aside and dealt with as one of the nuisances of daily life. Nuisances tend to, and can, anger and needlessly adversely occupy one's emotions for a good part of a day. In my interpretation, if it's not a death or near-death situation or grave health situation or illness of yourself or someone you love or is close to you, all other untoward circumstances that we face in daily life should be addressed with less anxiety and in varying degrees of less energy and emotional strain and drain. Life is full of problems; and untoward circumstances, interruptions, and more minor situations need not be allowed to upset me and elevate my emotions to the same or near the same level of anxiety, stress, and emotional drain experienced in situations that I feel truly do fall into a serious, near-death, or like situation.

It seems apparent to me that it is very difficult for others who have not shared the experience of facing death and coping with it to truly understand how this experience could and does change one's attitude toward life and how to deal with the ensuing problems after such a life-altering experience. Because of my seemingly more lighthearted (not to be misconstrued as irresponsible) attitude toward minor nuisances that I encounter since my cancers, and because I don't exhibit the same degree of anger or similar irate or emotional responses to problems of others, I have been accused by some close to me of being cold, having little feeling or compassion when they are upset, and raving about what I interpret to be a rather minor problem. I have tried a few times to explain my thinking and my attitude of setting aside more minor problems and just skimming over the little nuisances and treating them accordingly, but most people I have shared that philosophy with seemingly don't understand or comprehend my explanation. So I have come to the conclusion that perhaps only others who have shared such a life-threatening, near-death, or grave experience can grasp my explanation for seemingly being cold and less feeling or less compassionate in addressing the minor nuisances of life.

In a way, I feel far more free to enjoy life, having learned to not let all the challenging problems that arise on an almost daily basis consume my emotions or concern me. Consequently, I feel my life is fuller, and I am able to put a more positive attitude on situations than I had done in the past before my illnesses. I find that I see humor more readily in various situations than I had in the past. These attitudes are reflected in the events recalled throughout this book, and as a consequence, many instances and events in this book may appear to be fabricated or enhanced for effect. However, the events have been written as they occurred, without embellishments, although, in many instances, the occurrence may seem unbelievable.

21

About Traveling, Vacations, and Dealing with Adversity

*F*ollowing my recovery from my first cancer, I began to feel an urgency to pursue more of the adventures I had thus far thought of only fleetingly as events to pursue at some point in the future. The effects of having faced my mortality left me afraid that I might not have the leisure of putting things off indefinitely before pursuing adventures I had hoped to experience in my lifetime. I began to seriously plan to make some of those dreams reality sooner rather than later.

After the recurrence of my cancer, these thoughts accelerated, so that I did, in fact, begin to seriously pursue my adventures when I was able to bring them to fruition.

The next series of stories involve my travels from New York to California, a solo train trip, and a memorable trip to Hawaii, all of which were grossly interrupted. The stories demonstrate how I handled the situations by not allowing myself to dwell too long on the anger and anxiety caused by the events, and then to focus on finding solutions to my predicaments; I exercised my self-training of mental probing in order to find humor or purpose in the dilemmas and experiences, and then challenge myself to turn the events into positive experiences.

Handling untoward circumstances in this manner requires training oneself to adopt this way of thinking and put forth a concentrated effort to achieve a positive result. When I have been successful in practicing this philosophy, the outcome has been most rewarding.

*The following stories and travel experiences are
post-second-cancer events.*

22

Winter Travels from the East Coast to the West Coast

*T*his was an unbelievable attempt to travel from New York to Sacramento on December 28, 2015.

In my haste to make my reservation for my New York–Sacramento trip for my sister Val's birthday cruise on January 2, 2016, although I carefully allowed five days to travel in the event we had inclement weather delays from New York, I had forgotten my practice not to travel through Chicago in the winter months. Consequently, my fears of delays in Chicago came to fruition on this very eventful trip.

Monday, December 28, 2015

After a 4:30 a.m. pickup by Eric and his wife Mina, we arrived at LaGuardia Airport about 5:00 a.m., in plenty of time for my 6:30 a.m. flight. I got checked in (no TSA precheck available, so I had to go through the cumbersome regular baggage security check-in procedure of checking my bags at the counter, then moving my bags to the baggage drop before getting into the regular security line). The flight was fine, except the man sitting in the middle seat next to me seemed a little chatty, so I tried desperately to avoid conversation until halfway through the flight since I wanted to read. When I finally allowed myself to engage in conversation, there was no more reading time. He wanted to yak and yak, especially when he learned we had a common ancestry background. He was friendly, apparently visits New York often, and wanted to exchange phone numbers so he could touch bases on his New York visits. He was surprised when I would not share my phone number, since I advised him that I had zero time for socializing, as my work kept me very preoccupied. In fact, I explained that my close friends and I get together only once a year to celebrate all our birthdays together, because we are all so busy and preoccupied in our own individual lives with little time for socializing. Late in the flight, I did give him my landline number, suggesting that he at least could leave me a message there. Later, I was sorry that we had not exchanged cell numbers since we might have been able to assist each other in the hours of confusion that followed.

As we neared O'Hare International Airport, it seemed we were circling quite a bit. Then the captain spoke over the loudspeaker with an announcement that the Chicago airport had closed because of the snowstorm and we were being diverted to the Louisville, Kentucky, airport.

When we deplaned in Louisville, we were told we would be delayed for at least five hours before continuing on to Chicago. I went to grab a bite to eat. This was a rather small airport, and there were only two food vendors, a sandwich/deli counter and a regular full-service restaurant. Other planes began arriving from also being diverted. Soon, the lines at the two restaurants began growing, and I, along with my fellow passengers on my plane, were glad we were the first plane to be diverted. Over the ensuing hours, I think a total of seven to eight planes were diverted to this airport. The two food lines continued to extend along the length of the airport terminal, and customers began complaining that the sandwich shop was running out of food.

Well, needless to say, if you were able to secure a seat in the terminal, you were lucky and should not vacate it. Finally, at five o'clock in the evening, the people in my waiting area began to line up to reboard along the wall. After about twenty minutes, we saw the captain of the plane and several of the plane crew exit the plane and leave in the direction of the baggage claim area and the terminal exit. The eyes of all of those of us waiting in line grew questionable, as we commiserated that this was not a good sign. Sure enough, after about twenty minutes more, an announcement came in our waiting area that the crew who had come in with us had to leave because their shift had expired, and we must await a replacement crew. So we all settled down again for a long wait. Well, after about a half hour, an agent came on the loudspeaker and asked the crowd in the entire terminal to be silent; she said that she would not speak until all were quiet, since she had a very important announcement to make. Once the terminal had quieted down, the agent advised the crowd that planes would not be going to Chicago today, as that airport would not reopen today; also that there would be no flights leaving Louisville for the balance of the day; all planes for the day had been canceled, and there was no information available as to any flights that would be leaving Louisville before the end of the week (today was Monday). All were advised to go down to the baggage claim area to retrieve their baggage, then go through the security area to return here in order to make arrangements for their next available flight out of Louisville. Also, there were minimal, if any, buses that would become available to take passengers to Chicago. After another five minutes, a further announcement was made that there were no buses nor trains at all available out of Louisville for the balance of the day.

Rather than leave to claim my luggage as suggested, I (and other passengers) scrambled to get into line at the agents' counter to arrange for a flight out of Louisville. When my turn came, the agent advised that either (1) I could backtrack and catch a flight back east to New Jersey possibly in two days and try to get a flight to the West Coast from there or (2) she could book me on a flight out of Louisville on Friday (four days hence). I opted for this reservation, knowing my party cruise for my sister was scheduled for Saturday, but I felt at least I would have a definite reservation to fly on Friday. I was advised that the airline would not provide complimentary hotel accommodations, as this was not required in the event of a "weather delay." However, she could and did give me a discount voucher (termed a "distressed passenger" discount voucher). Before going to claim my luggage, I sat and made arrangements for a hotel room, as I knew the rooms would be quickly filling up. I grabbed a box of chicken to take, to avoid having to look for food at the hotel, since I intended to immediately get on the computer to try to arrange for an earlier flight out. Luckily, I claimed my baggage readily and found the complimentary hotel shuttle. The room was quite comfortable, which pleased me, since this might likely be my home for the next four days! (Thank God my credit cards were not maxed out. *A lesson for anyone traveling, regardless of how routine one may think his or her trip might be: always travel with good credit availability on your credit cards and always bring extra cash for emergencies!)*

Once I had settled into the room, I checked bus and train schedules to the West Coast. At first, I thought of checking a bus schedule to Chicago, in order to possibly get a connection there in the next day or two; but then I thought that to be a senseless thought, since I could end up waiting in the Chicago airport terminal for the next few days to get out as well. At least, I did have a decent, comfortable room here for $106 per night. I decided to hang on to my January 1, 2016, reservation until I could find something that made better sense than my current reservation. I called the airline, but after waiting a long time, I learned there were no earlier reservations available.

I was exhausted, so I bought a soda and ate my chicken, then nodded off. I awakened about three thirty in the morning and decided to call the airline again for a possible flight sooner than Friday. After about an hour on hold, I got a very nice agent on the phone who listened to my woeful tale and tried very hard to get me a flight. After much searching, she finally found one seat available going to San Francisco that morning, leaving at eight in the morning. I thanked the agent for her kindness and her patience in searching the computer to find this flight. It was now nearing six in the morning, so I had to scramble. I didn't know about the reliability of the shuttle or a taxi to the airport, and I didn't want to lose this reservation. I would call my sister from the airport once I was checked in. Luckily, there was an available bell captain who used his cart for my luggage. Again, luck was on my side since I was able to quickly get a taxi. When I reached the airport, the skycap was amazed, as he said I was one of the few people who got on a flight that day. I felt very fortunate. I made a call to my sister and was lucky to reach her right away.

Since I no longer had my early boarding status, I was one of the last people to board. I would go to San Francisco via Phoenix. I spotted a middle seat toward the front, where a man in the aisle seat and the lady next to the window were very animated in a discussion about dogs. When I sat down, I realized that the woman next to the window had a dog in a carrier at her feet. I feared the dog would be barking during the flight, and I wanted to jump up and ask for another seat, but I decided that was probably futile since the plane was packed.

As it turned out, the dog was incredibly well behaved. I wouldn't have known he was there had I not already seen him. The three of us in that row had animated continuous discussions about everything the entire trip. I felt sorry for anyone around us who wanted peace and quiet, because there was none of that. The man next to me talked nonstop the entire three-hour flight. As we were deplaning, I learned there was another dog in the row in front of me, unbeknownst to me. Those two dogs changed my opinion about dogs traveling on airplanes. They were both quieter than some children I've traveled with on planes.

I had called my sister, Val, as I was boarding my flight to arrange for her to pick me up. Unfortunately and regrettably, through all the confusion of the last day, I had not thought to call Gordy to update him, since he was to pick me up in Sacramento the day before. Gordy called me as I was waiting for Val to pick me up. I felt so badly that in all the commotion of the last thirty-five hours or so since leaving New York, I had not thought to call Gordy myself. I guess my sister had contacted Gordy for me yesterday. Gordy was always so good about making himself available to take me to and from the Sacramento airport any time of day whenever I flew in or out, and he was so good about arranging to pick me up Monday (yesterday) in Sacramento.

Thankfully, I reached my destination safe and sound, forty hours after leaving my New York home at four thirty the morning before.

23

Turning a Negative into a Positive:

A Flight Cancellation in Nashville Becomes a Positive Experience

*M*y nephew, radio announcer and DJ, Gordy died on May 24, 2017. Gordy, or the vibrant "Boomer Cruz," was a renowned and energetic voice to millions of his listeners as a radio announcer in several areas of the San Francisco Bay Area and also in Southern California. Included in his resume were San Francisco KSRY "Star FM"; KFGY "Froggy" 92.9 (Country) Santa Rosa; KROY (Rock), V101 Sacramento; KHYL V101.1 Sacramento; KKIS "Kiss FM" Concord; KCRK "The Creek" Walnut Creek; KTOM, V107FM and V109FM Salinas, and others. I have written a separate chapter "About Gordy," in which I have expanded on Gordy's many qualities and have also included a very poignant eulogy that highlights Gordy's wonderful and vibrant personality.

After a monthlong project with my sister, Val, to sort through Gordy's house and belongings, paying particular attention to protect his radio memorabilia and air checks, his various recordings from his library, and all his personal and sports memorabilia, I was ready to head back to New York.

My flight to New York required about a three-and-a-half-hour layover in Nashville, with a scheduled departure from Nashville at 4:15 p.m. At 4:20 p.m., an announcement at the gate indicated that the flight had been delayed but was due to arrive momentarily, and boarding was expected shortly thereafter following deplaning of the passengers on my arriving flight. At about four thirty, I received a text message that the flight had been canceled, with instructions to go to the agents' desk at the gate to make arrangements for another flight. As I was getting out of my seat to go to the gate agents' desk across the aisle, an announcement was made at the boarding gate, informing all waiting passengers that the flight had been canceled and everyone was instructed to go to the agents' desk to make other arrangements for another flight.

An immediate stampede ensued toward the agents' desk across the aisle, with people pushing ahead of me to get in line. Needless to say, contrary to my thinking that I'd be first in line, I ended up being about the tenth or twelfth person in line to reach a reservation agent. I ended up with a choice of a 6:45 a.m. flight the next day (Tuesday) to Newark or the same scheduled but aborted flight to LaGuardia at 4:45 p.m. on Tuesday. I opted for the next-day flight at 4:45 p.m. It was now about 5:30 p.m. Monday. Either way, I was advised that the airline would not provide a hotel at the airline's expense. The agent's excuse or reasoning was that the flight cancellation was not their fault, as the agent cited weather as the reason for the cancellation. The agent advised me that the air traffic controller in New York canceled all flights into the New York area (JFK, LaGuardia, and Newark) because of weather. However, accounts from people in the New York area were that the weather was normal—there were no extreme weather conditions. It came to my mind later on that evening that the cancellations were likely due to a terror threat and that the air traffic controller did not want to publicize that. (Someone else had suggested possible computer problems.) **Note:** As I mentioned in the previous chapter, I was told that if cancellations are due to weather conditions, the airlines are not responsible for providing overnight accommodations for displaced passengers.

Well, I finally got a reservation for a room at the Inn (although I learned later that it was not the closest one to the airport). I ended up befriending my cab driver Jolene, who was an absolute doll. In talking, we somehow came upon a subject that brought about her sharing with me a near-death experience she had had years ago. She described the experience as being *engulfed with an indescribable beautiful, serene, calm sense about her. It was a feeling of pure joy, contentment, love, and peace; and she was totally immersed in this indescribable beautiful sense.* I was so in awe and inspired to hear her speak of such an experience. Having felt the loss to death of my firstborn nephew, my baby brother, and my ex-husband, all in the last three years, I felt very close to death. I often have thoughts of dying and trying to imagine what it would be like on the other side. I really was moved by hearing of Jolene's remarkable experience, and I thanked her for sharing such a moving, joyous recollection with me.

It became apparent at the first inn that we needed to go farther to their second location. Once we arrived, Jolene came in to collect her fare directly from the desk clerk rather than have me pay first and then ask for reimbursement. She was so considerate. (When I made my reservation and had inquired whether the hotel had an airport shuttle, the reservation/desk clerk indicated that the hotel did not have an airport shuttle but that the hotel would reimburse my taxi fare to and from the hotel.)

We bade adieu, and I took Jolene's business card so I could call her if I wanted her services to return to the airport tomorrow. She said I should, however, definitely go to Downtown Broadway tonight, where all the clubs would have live bands (country and western, of course)—*an absolute must-see*, according to Jolene. This sentiment was repeated by the hotel desk clerk and one other guest.

I had multiple problems with my room, and after about an hour or more of trying to correct the problems, I was assigned another room. I was thankful to be able to get another room, since as the evening wore on, rooms were filling up from so many passengers displaced from flight cancellations.

At long last, after the last five hours of anxiety and frustration, I was able to sit and relax. I really wanted to go to Downtown Broadway and listen to live country and western music, but I was too exhausted. I thought I would lie down and take a quick rest, then head out. Unfortunately, so unlike me, I did not set my alarm to wake up after an hour or so. Consequently, I awakened at one thirty in the morning and figured it was really too late to head down to Broadway. I was very disappointed, yet I knew that if I had not had a little rest, I could not have gone downtown anyway. So I set my alarm to get up in time to catch breakfast the next morning. I experienced an additional problem, though. For some reason, my cell phone charger shorted out when I plugged it in, and consequently, I was unable to recharge my phone. So I was careful to limit my phone use in hopes that my remaining usage would last until I got home.

When I awoke the next morning, a brilliant idea came to mind. I could not shake the disappointment of not having gone to Downtown Broadway to listen to the live country-western bands. So I thought at the very least, I could go to the Broadway and walk around to have a look at the area in the daylight. That way, I could at least satisfy myself that I had gone down to see the famous Downtown Broadway of Nashville, the Country Capital of the World. In this way, I could at least turn the whole mishap of my canceled flight into a positive result.

I went down to have breakfast, made arrangements for my 2:00 p.m. shuttle service back to the airport, and inquired of the desk clerk regarding what times the Downtown Broadway clubs opened. He informed me that many began opening with live music at eleven o'clock in the morning. So I got my breakfast and took it to my room. I then called Jolene, my taxi driver from yesterday, and made arrangements for her to pick me up at ten thirty to go downtown.

I suggested to Jolene that it might be difficult for her to commit to picking me up at ten thirty, depending on where she was around that time, but she assured me it would be fine. Sure enough, at about ten thirty, I received a text from Jolene that she somehow had taken a wrong turn and had gotten lost with her last customer but she was back on track and would be there soon. Because of her delay, she would charge me only ten dollars.

Jolene arrived around a quarter to eleven, and we were on our way. She said she would not charge me at all. She was insistent on taking no money at all and wouldn't even take a tip. She said she would collect her tip later when she picked me up to take me back to the hotel. I recounted my cell phone charger incident to Jolene. Fortunately, Jolene had a car charger that I could use to charge my phone as we drove. Jolene dropped me right in front of Legends, the famous nightclub (Tootsie's was next door, but there was no music playing). Jolene had given me a quick rundown of the area as we drove up Broadway. She suggested I walk Second Avenue—lots of shops.

Jolene and I made arrangements for her to pick me up at one thirty for the return trip to the hotel. After Jolene dropped me off, I stopped for a minute at Legends and planned to return after a quick walk. I walked back to Second Avenue and stopped in to check out a pricey hat shop. Then, as I headed back to Legends, I stopped to check out a few places that were playing live music. I decided I would later come back to the Copper Roof for lunch and more live music before going back to the hotel.

Legends was great live music. I had two beers, I think—maybe a third. Then I tipped the bartender and the group playing and headed on back to the Copper Roof. I was quite tipsy on my two to three beers and stopped to catch my bearings. I ordered a great hamburger and fries and another beer (the music was better at Legends). At about one fifteen, I opened my phone to call Jolene, and she had texted me, inquiring where I was. I paid my bill, had my remaining food packed to go, and headed back to Legends to meet Jolene. I was feeling my drinks, all right.

I was elated at having the presence of mind to think of coming down to Broadway before heading back to the airport. I was quite proud of myself and no longer felt that I had wasted an opportunity to see and enjoy the famous "Broadway of Nashville". I would have been kicking myself for a long time, had I not done so.

Jolene picked me up and brought me back to the hotel. When we arrived, we were informed that the shuttle had not come and really was not expected, so the hotel was willing to pay Jolene to take me to the airport. Jolene was delighted since the hotel clerk paid her eighteen dollars; she said she had intended to charge only ten dollars. Coupled with the generous payment I gave her, she was quite happy. I was so fortunate to meet and become acquainted with Jolene. She was truly a gracious, kind, and compassionate person. Our world would be a better place with more people of her caliber in it.

All in all, what was a real negative happenstance of a canceled flight out of Nashville turned into a real positive, with an overnight stay and a tour of the world-famous Nashville and Downtown Broadway, the Country Capital of the World. (Had I opted for the 6:45 a.m. flight, I would have missed out on this little minitour of a fabulous city.)

24

Fabulous Solo Birthday Holiday:

New York City–New Orleans

(French Quarter) and Return

For so many years since I had returned from my six-month vacation in Europe, I'd had a desire to take a long train ride in the United States. I so enjoyed many of my train trips going across the European continent from Venice to Lisbon, and at that time, I thought I would like to see the United States by train upon my return home.

It wasn't until many years later that I happened upon an Amtrak schedule and learned of a direct train from New York to New Orleans, with no train change. I decided to make this trip my long-awaited train excursion in the United States.

This trip was one of the most taxing of my travel experiences. I really had to exert much mental probing throughout this experience to keep my anger and anxiety in check and try to find positive elements during this trip.

At one in the afternoon, I went downstairs to catch a cab. It was highly unusual that there were no taxis waiting around for possible customers. So I walked to Second Avenue to get a cab. The slow taxi ride across town was unnerving, with numerous unsuccessful attempts to cross Fifth Avenue to the West Side. Finally, the taxi driver informed me that my best option was to get off at Thirty-Fourth Street and Fifth Avenue and walk the long three avenue blocks to the train station, with luggage in tow.

Aboard the train, I got a window seat, and a heavyset male sat next to me. He was traveling to Greensboro, North Carolina, and would not exit the train until midnight. Because I did not want to give up my more scenic window seat, at night I ended up sitting in the club car quite a bit to avoid having to disturb my seatmate for frequent bathroom usage. Since he was scheduled to exit the train at midnight, I could then make use of his vacated seat and I would have my window seat to enjoy the scenery during the daytime travel hours. All in all, I was quite happy with the train ride and comfort.

The scenery going south was lush, with trees and vegetation surrounding most of our route. The sunrises and sunsets were incredibly picturesque, with vibrant hues of orange, purples, and rose tones spanning across the skies. Just before New Orleans, we traversed a very long, twenty-mile-plus, low causeway bridge, which we skirted right along the surface of the lake. I learned that this was *Lake Pontchartrain*, apparently built in 1956 to cut travel time by fifty minutes from north shore communities to New Orleans. It was an absolutely beautiful ride, a very majestic view of the placid, calm lake in all directions, like a mirror, devoid of breakers to interrupt the calmness of the lake. I was amazed and quite astonished at the length of this bridge and how close we were paralleling the surface of the lake. It was about a twenty-two-minute crossing at train speed. After the long bridge and just outside New Orleans, the train slowed to a crawl of about five miles per hour for the last forty-five minutes of the ride. No announcement was given to explain the reason for the slow down.

We arrived in New Orleans about forty-five minutes late; our scheduled arrival was 7:32 p.m. I ended up getting one of the last taxis available.

After I checked in at the hotel, the porter lit up my nicely furnished room and opened the drapes, only to find that my window was facing a brick wall right outside the window, only about six feet away from my window. Noticing my displeasure with this situation, the porter suggested we go back down to see about a room change.

After much discussion and much research on the part of the desk clerk, I was able to make a room change without the refrigerator and other amenities at the same rate I had. At least, my window faced a courtyard, not a brick building just six feet out. The clerk advised me that the only rooms available in the computer for the next day were premium rooms at much higher rates, but he suggested I check early the following morning for any possibilities for a room change to my liking.

The next morning at a quarter to nine, I went to the front desk regarding changing my room. For the first fifteen minutes of searching the computer, it looked as if I must stay in my room or pay for an upgrade, but persistency paid off, and the clerk finally found room number 219 opening up because the guest standing next to me was moving out of the room. The woman said it was a nice room. So at nine thirty, it was settled that I would move once the room had been cleaned, hopefully in a couple of hours. I decided to go to the drugstore for some wine and snacks for the room, and along the way, I bought a beautiful purple T-shirt embroidered with "New Orleans—French Quarter," which would become my souvenir of this trip. My room was not ready until after one in the afternoon.

I was pleased when I entered a very comfortable, charming room with a little refrigerator and was pleasantly surprised when I saw French doors that opened onto a balcony facing a courtyard. The U-shaped courtyard was lined with three floors of rooms, each with scrolled wrought-iron lining each of the balconies. The whole courtyard was very charming and pleasant to view. After settling in, I could finally get on with my day. I headed for Harrah's Casino, a walk of about eight blocks. I got to the casino at two thirty in the afternoon and played until a quarter after five, as I had to return to the hotel to get ready to see Neil Diamond at the Smoothie King Center that night. I was lucky to catch a trolley back to where Val and Bob (my sister and brother-in-law) and I had gotten beignets (a French fritter) two or three years earlier. I ordered a fried shrimp platter to go and hurriedly walked back to my room through the colorful French Quarter as it was beginning to come alive for the evening, jazz music echoing through the streets.

I had my fried shrimp dinner and got dressed to attend the Neil Diamond concert at eight o'clock. I was so exhausted from the whole room change ordeal and lack of sleep that I nodded off for about forty-five minutes. I awakened at a quarter after seven and jumped up to get ready and went to grab a cab. Traffic was very heavy around the Smoothie King Center; I arrived at a quarter to eight for the eight o'clock concert. I was surprised at the number of people lining up to buy food and drinks right around eight, the supposed beginning of the concert. I bought a bottle of water and was surprised when the vendor removed the bottle cap and disposed of it—I was advised by the vendor that removal of the bottle caps was an arena regulation. (I guess even bottle caps can be weaponized.)

It was a fabulous concert. Neil Diamond's performance was vibrant and exciting. He sounded probably as good as he sounded fifty years earlier (this was his fifty-year anniversary concert tour). I guess he must have sung at least twenty to twenty-five songs in a two-hour concert. He had a great backup group—very similar, I thought, to Elvis's backup group at his concerts, less the choir. I believe that backup groups are important to the successful sound of the performer. Neil Diamond is more easy listening as opposed to Elvis's strong baritone and projecting voice and sound, but because of the backup band, singers, and instruments, Neil Diamond's sounds, to me, were a close second or third to Elvis's sounds. "Sweet Caroline" was his last song, and it played for a good ten minutes or more. The crowd was roaring and in heaven. This was after the first curtain call, and I had already gone down one level below my level to get ahead of the crowd. After "Sweet Caroline," I rushed out and got one of the first taxis. The driver waited to hail another couple, who happened to have taken their first train ride from Texas to attend the concert. It was a pleasant and informative ride back to the French Quarter, since I wanted to learn a little about the train service from Texas. (Early on, I had entertained the thought of arranging a family reunion in New Orleans in the French Quarter, and one of my brothers and his wife would probably be taking the train from Texas.)

Back at the hotel, I stopped in at Ma's Hideout for my last drink before retiring. I bade adieu to the bartender and said I'd be back the next night, but I never made it back the next night. I wanted to take a late-night walk around the French Quarter, but I was quite exhausted and felt a little unsteady on my feet and thought better of it.

The next morning at breakfast, a woman told me it was supposed to rain all day. I headed out to fulfill my mission of checking out my hotel's sister hotels and get my beignets for the train ride tomorrow. The balance of the day, I wanted to stay in and enjoy my room. Just as I was starting out, it started to rain. On Bourbon Street, there were many balconies overhead that offered shelter from the rain. I found and checked out the three sister hotels I had gone to find. While wandering about, I found myself in front of the beignet place, so I went in and secured those for the morning. Having finished my mission to locate the sister hotels, I stopped in a pub/restaurant on the corner from my hotel to check the menu (probably a good burger place). If the shrimp fry was other than popcorn shrimp, I might opt for dinner here rather than weathering the rain to find another restaurant. The waitress informed me that the shrimp frys on almost all the menus in the French Quarter were usually popcorn shrimp. She did, however, against the house rules of recommending other restaurants, steer me in the direction of a seafood restaurant, where she thought I might enjoy a good regular shrimp dinner, and it was only two blocks from my hotel. I took a walk to the restaurant to check out the menu—an excellent lunch menu but served only until three in the afternoon. After three o'clock, prices skyrocketed for the same menu. So I vowed to return before three since it was now only late morning.

At a quarter to two in the afternoon, huge thunderstorms came pouring down. I was glad to be back in my room watching the rain pour down on my little balcony. By a quarter to three, the storms had subsided a bit, so I headed over to the seafood restaurant after grabbing a rain poncho at the front desk. The "mate's platter" with fried shrimp and oysters—absolutely the best oysters I've had in probably two decades—was not only delicious but an excellent bargain. I placed an order of oysters to take back to my room and ended up eating them about an hour later.

The storm strengthened, along with strong winds. The balance of the day was rainy and stormy. I was thankful that I had fulfilled my mission of going to the casino yesterday and had planned to stay in today anyway, so I was not too unhappy that it was storming. I repacked my things and just enjoyed reading and watching the rain come down on my balcony. I had planned to go back to Ma's Hideout cocktail lounge downstairs, but I was still quite tired and kept nodding off all day until it was ten thirty at night, really quite late since I must rise and shine tomorrow for my taxi pickup at a quarter to six in the morning to go to the Amtrak station. I finished packing and just enjoyed the TV and the news. At about midnight, the TV went down because of the storm.

The Return Journey Home

May 4, 2017, 4:15 a.m.

Rise and shine—I had reserved a taxi for about a quarter to six to be at the Amtrak station by a quarter after six. Apparently, the front desk had not called in my taxi order to the valet, since there was no record of my reservation. So the valet, Marlene, had to call for a taxi—luckily it came in five to ten minutes. The cabdriver did not even get out at the hotel pickup to open the trunk or help with my bags. The hotel porter assisted me, and I thanked and tipped her accordingly. At the station, the driver unloaded my bags, so I did give him a tip, although I debated about giving him anything over the fare amount because of his earlier attitude.

The train was late in arriving to New Orleans by about forty-five minutes. However, it turned around immediately (to my surprise without a checkout period of the maintenance status of the train). I guess we departed New Orleans at eight o'clock. Sometime in the late morning before reaching Tuscaloosa, there apparently was a train emergency, wherein we had to wait for the emergency to be cleared before proceeding. Finally, after almost two hours, we were on our way to Tuscaloosa.

Then, sometime in the middle of the night (I fell asleep just before nine at night and awakened just before two in the morning), I realized we had completely stopped. I and the other passengers seated around me sat there wondering what was going on. There were no announcements, and no crew could be found anywhere for close to two hours. Then we began to see conductors and engineers exiting and entering the train and milling around the outside. Finally, a passenger learned that apparently, when we were coming around a bend, there was a large tree lying across the tracks. The train, unable to avoid the obstacle, hit the tree, causing damage to the two engines. Thank God the impact did not cause our train to go off the tracks or tilt off the tracks. It seemed rather incredulous to me and the others that none of us felt any jolt or unusual movement of the train when it impacted the tree obstacle on the tracks.

At this point, I checked into my anxiety compass and decided that since my arrival in New York was somewhat flexible for the next twenty hours, I should just chill out and take stock of all the commotion.

Well, as the explanation goes, there was only one track shared by trains going in both directions at that section of the tracks. Our accident caused a long delay of all traffic going in both directions. We had to await a larger locomotive to tow us to a two-track section of the railroad so other trains could continue on their journey. Once we were towed, we had to wait for two more freight trains to come and bring us two more engines to replace our damaged two engines. The two new engines were installed, and we learned that we were currently outside Clemens, South Carolina, and I calculated that to be another fifteen hours' train ride to Manhattan.

Finally, after seven hours, thirty-five minutes, we were again on our way at 11:40 a.m.; expected arrival in Manhattan was a quarter after two in the morning. *Wrong!* More unexpected stops would occur south of Alexandria and Washington, DC, with no explanations or announcements.

We finally reached Penn Station in Manhattan about six thirty in the morning. This had been a forty-seven-hour train ride for a scheduled twenty-nine-hour trip. I felt badly for the two men sitting across the aisle from me. They were scheduled to attend a conference yesterday. They not only missed a day of the conference but also lost their hotel reservation for last night.

25

An Enchanted Island Vacation with a Whopping Ending

This trip brought back memories of the events of 9/11 in New York.

On Thursday, January 4, 2018, a huge storm hit New York City; eleven hundred flights were canceled. I was hoping that the airport would reopen the next day, Friday, and get back on track, since I was due to fly to Hawaii for one week on Saturday. On Friday, I checked the status of my flight several times with the airline and got a go, so I proceeded to get my boarding passes and hoped that things would go as scheduled. Again early the next morning, I checked for the status and again got a go.

It wasn't until I was checked in and at the gate that there was a notice on the gate status board that the flight was delayed for an hour; subsequently it was delayed again and ended up actually taking off three hours after the scheduled flight time. However, it was a smooth ten-hour flight. Once in Hawaii, I was able to get a shuttle to the time-share hotel and readily obtain my room key from the security guard.

It was so nice to be back in our time share. The unit was nicely appointed with all the comforts, fully equipped with kitchen utensils and a balcony, and this time with an ocean view rather than a mountain view. I was a bit exhausted but went on to the little neighborhood supermarket so I'd be set to hang out with all my necessities for as long as I wanted. This was, after all, intended to be a working week—time to work on this book and hopefully get it finished or as close to finished as possible. By the time I returned to the room, I was beginning to feel the effects of having been on the go for the last twenty hours and just conked out after putting away my goodies.

The next day, Sunday, at one in the afternoon, I went to the management office to get checked in. I was still quite tired, feeling the effects of the cold I had been fighting, and went back to the room to relax a bit before going out for a walk around the area and the beach. I ended up falling asleep in front of the television for about five to six hours. I guess I needed the rest. It wasn't until Monday that I actually felt up to and began to do my writing. I arranged the kitchen table so I could also see and watch the TV and the news while I wrote. Now I was comfortable and ready to begin my task. I had all my provisions and decided that I could go on for hours on end and any time of the day or night with my writing. I was as happy as a clam. For the next five days, I would do my writing and take a break at some point to take a walk around the area and the beach and enjoy the weather and the surroundings. Despite Waikiki having grown into a huge shopping center and hotel/convention area, I found it very pleasing. The shops and stores and walkways all along Kalakaua and Kuhio Boulevards and the surroundings have been pleasantly designed, and of course, flora and tropical greenery abound throughout the area. A walk along the beach with the water lapping at your feet is such an enjoyable, soothing experience. The walkway on the street along the beach lined with island flora and swaying palm trees afforded many stopping points to just sit and watch the water or enjoy a sunset. So I made it a point to fit in some time in my day or night to enjoy this enchanting island.

For the next four days, I continued my writing and afforded myself at least one break a day just to enjoy being on this lovely island. It wasn't until Friday that I allowed myself the luxury of actually taking the time to just sit and enjoy a leisurely meal in a restaurant. I had had enough takeout and cooking in the room the last four days so as to really focus on my project of writing my book. Finally on Friday, after I had completed my breakfast, all of a sudden the water was shut off; luckily this didn't happen while I was in the shower with soap all over my body. I thought it would be turned back on in a short period of time. Anyway, I learned that the running water would not resume until sometime around three o'clock. I was not pleased with this revelation, since I didn't recall any forewarning that the water would be shut off. When I finally went out, I did see a sign at the elevator banks downstairs regarding the intended water shutoff. I was surprised that I could have missed seeing the sign, but I guess when I had gone out and returned the day before, an elevator had just come down, and I must have run to catch the elevator and therefore missed the water shutoff notice.

This being my last full day, I planned to at least have dim sum at my favorite dim sum restaurant before leaving Hawaii, and also to go see what was going on at the Beachview Restaurant, which my sister and I learned was closing, with the last day of business to be the day after we left Hawaii last September. The Beachview was a favorite restaurant of my deceased brother Ted, and I always think of him and the time he, my sister, Val, brother-in-law Bob, and I came to enjoy a great meal here a few years back when we all came to Hawaii together to spend a week at our time shares. Ted was an avid steak eater, and the Beachview specialized in a grill-your-own steak grilling counter with an added salad and condiment buffet. I decided I would go back for an early dinner and check out the new restaurant that replaced the Beachview.

I headed on over and decided to get my dim sum to go, so I could enjoy the time on the beach a bit on this last day. I stopped at the downstairs dim sum place to see how late they served, since I knew they would soon stop serving the dim sum. I was informed that I could return in another fifty minutes to place an order before the kitchen closed at two in the afternoon. I went across to the beach to my favorite spot and sat on the stone beach wall and just enjoyed the sun. I was in my street clothes, as I had not intended to bask on the beach. Before heading back to the restaurant to place my order, I walked along the water, just to dip my feet a bit and to say goodbye to the beach for this trip. Then I headed back to place my order for dim sum. I went to buy some macadamia nuts to take home, then headed back to my room. Since I had eaten breakfast not too long ago, I decided to save the dim sum for a late night snack. Then I did some packing and read a bit of my notes.

At about four o'clock, I decided to take a walk over to the hotel on the beach where the Beachview Restaurant had operated (I believe for more than thirty years). I had no idea what to expect with the replacement restaurant, but I intended to check it out. The setting of the restaurant was so refreshing. It was a veranda-type setting, no glass windows, just the open air along the beach. The restaurant was right on the beach, and in the evening one could sit right at the dinner table and enjoy watching the sunset, the cool ocean breeze whispering by as the sun slowly descended into the horizon, lighting the sky with glorious hues of orange, rose, and lavender. As it descended, it slowly left behind the darkness of a summer's eve with softly blowing breezes. It was the most strikingly beautiful setting. I was so pleased to see that the restaurant configuration had not been changed, and I asked if I might have a table along the beachside opening. Since it was early, there was not too much resistance to this, though the beachside tables were settings for four people. I ordered my mai tai and brought out some of my manuscript to read. I enjoyed this beautiful setting overlooking the water, and the soft cool breezes. As the evening approached, I watched the sun setting over the water, and I marvelled at the beautiful hues of purples, orange and rose as the sun descended. Soon I noticed the restaurant was beginning to fill up, so I paid my bill and left the waiter a very hefty tip for letting me enjoy my drinks and time here without feeling rushed. He was very appreciative and thanked me.

On Saturday, January 13, 2018, as I was cleaning up the kitchen and preparing to take my shower, a loud alarm came on my cell phone with a text, reading in part: "*Ballistic missile heading to Hawaii, due momentarily. Seek shelter. This is not a drill!*" On the news there were instructions to stay away from windows; if driving, to stop and seek shelter in a building if possible, otherwise lie flat on the ground. The warnings repeated continuously. It was a beautiful sunny day. *(My mind returned back to the memory of 9/11 in New York City to another beautiful, cloudless, sunny day before the tragic, horrific events of that day. But for now, back to the present.)* I closed the wooden louvered blinds on my balcony door and windows and on my bedroom window. Then I stepped away from the windows and balcony door as far as possible to the opposite side of the room while I listened for further word or news on the television. I was listening for sirens, which I thought surely would be blasting throughout the area. After about thirty-five minutes or so, there came an announcement on the television and on my cell phone that the earlier warning was a false alarm, that there was no threat of a ballistic missile coming our way. I breathed a huge sigh of relief but wondered, as did the commentators on the television, why it took the thirty-five minutes or so to post the false alarm. After listening further to the news, it was apparent that we could finally go about our business. It was eight thirty in the morning, and I hustled to finalize my packing and get ready to vacate my unit, since I was scheduled to fly back to the mainland at two thirty in the afternoon and had an airport shuttle scheduled to pick me up at a quarter after eleven. Meanwhile, my luggage was a bit heavier than I wanted to handle, so I gathered some of the heavier items I could fit in a large-size box to mail to my sister's house in Vallejo, California. Then, at nine thirty, I vacated my room and took my luggage to hold in the management office while I ran to the post office in the office/shopping center a block away from the hotel to mail my goods. I returned to the management office in good time to gather my luggage and await my scheduled shuttle service at the front of the hotel.

All was good. I arrived at the airport in good time and went through the cumbersome procedure of dealing with the kiosks to print my luggage tags, then take my luggage to the agent at the conveyor belt to clear it for transport. That done, I was ready to go through the security checkpoint en route to the gate, but I had ample time to sit and relax a bit before doing so. I had some food I had packed, and to my dismay, about three bottles of liquid to either digest or discard. I was lucky enough to find a vacant seat at the far end of this congested, confusing area, and I sat and consumed some of my food and most of the liquid I had packed. That done, I went to the restroom to discard the remaining liquids and then went through the security checkpoint.

When I arrived at the terminal seven days earlier, as I was walking to the baggage claim area with two of the other passengers who had been on my flight, we happened upon (by accident) a terminal shuttle bus, which drove us to the baggage claim area and apparently circled the terminal on a regular basis to bring people back and forth from the security checkpoint terminal to the departing gates and back to the baggage claim area. I had taken note of this so I could take advantage of this shuttle on my return flight back to the mainland. For those unfamiliar with the Honolulu airport, there are as many as, I believe, sixty-five or so gates to traverse from the security checkpoint. I had seen in the Hawaiian Airlines magazine on the plane on my inbound flight a chart of the Honolulu airport terminal. In a description of the terminal, it actually detailed the approximate times it would take to walk from the security checkpoint to the various gates and gave approximate walking times of up to twenty to twenty-five minutes to walk to the farther gates, numbered in the sixties. So it really makes sense that they have shuttles that transport passengers back and forth from the gates to the security and baggage claim areas.

Since I was scheduled to depart from gate 62, I took advantage of my newfound information regarding the shuttles and was very pleased with myself that I had learned of the shuttle service. (Although I have been to the Honolulu airport probably about six times in the last few years, I had not known of this service on my previous trips.) Unfortunately, I had an accident when departing the shuttle bus and fell from the last step. It was a foolish mistake; I should have put my hand-carried bag on the ground first, before stepping down, instead of doing both simultaneously. As people helped me up and asked if I was all right, I said I was okay, although I immediately felt pain in my right foot. (My thought was that if I sought medical attention then, I likely would be quite delayed, would miss my flight, would have to rebook—and with the emergency events of this morning, my guess was that flights might likely be filling up with vacationers eager to return to the mainland—and I had already relinquished my hotel accommodations and would have to deal with that.) I was, however, able to walk, so I felt certain that I had not broken any bones and could hopefully manage first to get back to the mainland and then address this problem. I had mistakenly thought that there would be food vendors near my gate and had opted to buy my bottle of water for the plane ride at the gate area. Unfortunately I saw no food vendors nearby. I was able to walk another two or three gates back and found a kiosk stand with snacks and drinks, so I was able to purchase my bottle of water and hobbled back to my gate. After I had returned to the gate, I noticed a little alcove at the back end of the gate that had vending machines selling only water.

Well, thank God, the flight went well, and I did make it back to Oakland on the mainland. Thereafter, I hobbled around, alternately icing and then putting heating pads on my foot. I began to feel a nagging pain and went to a foot doctor who x-rayed my foot and advised me that I had broken a bone on the outer section of my foot. He explained the importance of keeping my foot totally immobile and offered me a choice of having a cast put in place or wearing a large boot, which could be removed at night. So for the next month, I hobbled around while wearing my big black boot!

Yes, this was an enchanted island vacation with a whopping ending!

Part Two
Very Personal Chapters and Expression of Deep Sentiments

The next chapters I'd like to share with my readers are quite personal and express very deep sentiments.

I believe the reader may gain a little more understanding of me as a person; and the sentiments, thoughts, and expressions may bring together a more wholesome insight into the events that have transpired throughout the chapters of this book.

26

Cruisin' Cruisin' (Post-Cancer #2)

I remember with such fond memories the excitement and thrill in the planning and actual event of our very first family reunion cruise in October 2000.

My siblings Ted, Max (spouse Lana), and Jim (spouse Poppy) had not experienced a truly remarkable vacation cruise, and my sister, Val (spouse Bob), had been on one or two short cruises. Otherwise, thus far the closest they had come to cruising was through my relayed experiences of luxury-line cruising.

Therefore, when I first thought of having a family reunion cruise, I was so excited and thrilled to have my siblings experience what I considered to be the ultimate vacation experience. By this time, I believe I had already taken roughly ten cruises on my own, and I loved the experience. From my very first cruise with two lady friends when I lived in Concord, I thought what a wonderful and affordable way to experience how the other half (the wealthy and financially secure population) lived, at least for seven days. I didn't have to make my bed, and my bed was turned down in the evening. I would leave my cabin during the day, and when I returned at night, my cabin had been cleaned, straightened, and put back in order, with fresh towels, drinking glasses, and toiletries refreshed.

And for the first time, I felt "this is how the wealthy people live." And, I thought, for a very reasonable roughly $1,000, I had this beautiful experience. (Prices have increased substantially since I took my first cruise.)

Around 1998 to 1999, I had gone back to live in Northern California and opened a retail boutique. One day, my sister and I were discussing having a one-week reunion of all us siblings and were trying to decide where to put this reunion together, since we would all be coming from three states: California, Texas, and New York. My sister suggested that we plan the reunion at my brother Jim and his wife's place in Texas. I expressed how unfair it would be for them or any one of us hosting such a reunion because that family would be saddled with the burden of preparation, shopping, cooking, cleanup, and so on; they would be exhausted from tending to eight people (five siblings and three spouses) and would not enjoy the reunion as would the others, who would be essentially relaxing for the week.

I remembered my cruising experiences and how wonderful and fun-filled the week on board the cruises were. I thought that a cruise would be very conducive to a family reunion, so that all would enjoy themselves and no particular person or persons would be overburdened with the necessary work that would be required for such a reunion at any one of our homes. A cruise setting would be ideal; all could do as they wished during the day—take an excursion, read, swim, sit by the pool, onboard ship activities during sea days, and so on. One could snack or have room service when hungry; and at night, we would all join together in the dining room and share our day's events. If up and about at midnight, one could partake of the midnight buffet. I envisioned the experience of a carefree week of total relaxation and socializing with one another and enjoying seven dress-up dinners together with no other worries, and I wanted to share such an experience with my siblings. There would be the added excitement of this being a first cruise for my brothers Ted, Max, and Jim and their spouses. We would select a big luxurious cruise ship, large enough for all to wander about and do as they pleased. I broached the subject with my sister. She was very reluctant, stating that there were a couple of our siblings who would not be able to afford to go on the cruise. I stressed that if they knew about the cruise ahead of time, they could save their money over the next eighteen months, and all five siblings and spouses would be able to attend. (I was prepared to help with costs for the two siblings who might not be able to save enough.) So we discussed it with our other siblings and began our planning. All were excited about this upcoming event.

Thus began a wonderful year and a half of planning, and the *excitement began*!

I began researching the various itineraries and discussed the possible itineraries and various ports with my sister. We opted for sailing on board the new *Viceroy*, the newest and largest ship of the Canary Cruises fleet, sailing from Miami to Grand Cayman, Cozumel, and Jamaica. We decided having shore days between sea days would be smart in case one of us would not fare well on multiple sea days.

Then I researched and compiled information on the various excursions available when the ship would dock at the various islands.

Since most of our group were first-time cruisers, I prepared several write-ups, including passport requirements; port check-in procedures; what to expect upon first boarding the ship; dressing for night dinners; ladies to bring an extra wrap for windy nights on deck; what to pack (motion sickness wristbands in case needed), and making sure to pack in their hand-carries all medications and necessary toiletries and a complete change of clothing in the event of loss of luggage; and other helpful hints, such as packing a snack for the plane since meals were not necessarily served. I wrote instructions regarding meeting their shuttle to the ship after staying the night in an expense-included overnight hotel in Miami. Everyone heeded my suggestions, and consequently everyone came well prepared, which made for a more comfortable, enjoyable week.

I was so excited about our cruise that I talked about it with my assistant Zena at my boutique. She was very envious and commiserated that she would never ever be able to have such an experience, that she was destined to never move or leave the area. I explained to Zena what the trip would cost her and prodded her to save her money over the next eighteen months, and then she'd be able to join us. At any rate, the initial deposit was $250, which would hold her reservation until three months prior to the cruise, when final payment would be due. The more we discussed it, the more Zena began to see the possibility of her actually joining us on this fabulous cruise and realizing a dream to actually get out of the area and do something absolutely amazing with her life. We began getting excited together at the idea of her coming along on our cruise/reunion. Zena became convinced to make it happen and to change the doomed course of her life.

Thereafter began periods of excitement in our boutique as Zena and I would discuss our upcoming cruise.

We also invited our aunt, who was the widow of my father's brother Dan. At the time, my aunt was a vibrant, bubbly seventy-three-year-old. Earlier in her life, she and my uncle had experienced the painful death of their only child, who died of leukemia at the age of four and a half. Prior to Janie's illness and death, my aunt was very easygoing and prone to laughter. This characteristic left her for many years, as she and my uncle mourned the death of their child. Years later, following the death of my uncle, my aunt took steps to enjoy her forced independence. First, my brother Ted helped her to learn to drive a car, so she was able to get around on her own. She began traveling around the United States and abroad with various friends and relations. By the time of our family cruise, she had been well traveled, her joyous personality had long since revived, and having her with us added to our overall enjoyment.

Our first cruise sailed out of Miami, with an overnight stay in Miami for those coming from California. I can only imagine the excitement and swelling of the hearts of my siblings and their spouses when the bus from the hotel in Miami rounded the bend on the hill and they caught the first glimpse of the "big, beautiful cruise liner" that was to be our ship and their home for the next seven days. I was thrilled just seeing it myself, so I can well imagine the excitement of all the others.

I boarded the ship with my friend Bella, and then I took the shuttle from the ship to the airport to go meet my brother Jim and his wife Poppy to ensure that they made it on time to board the ship. (My brother was known to miss timetables when boarding a plane, and I didn't want to take any chance that he and his wife would miss the sailing of the ship.) When the three of us got on board the *Viceroy*, we found the others near the Lido deck, where I had given instructions for all to meet for the actual ship's sailing. We had a photo-op on deck after sailing, and this photo is one of our most cherished siblings photos. (For some reason, my brother Ted was on the other side of the ship when we sailed, but he joined us as we were sailing; I guess I had given instructions to meet on the opposite side of the ship, so he met us just a short while after the actual sailing.)

We decided that there would be a specific table (if available) in an area on the Lido deck where, during the cruise, if anyone was looking for one of our cruise members, he or she should be able to find one of our cruise group to join. It was such a wonderful, carefree experience, and yet one could always find another person to meet up with if desiring company. I had also made a list of each member of our group and the corresponding cabin numbers so any one of us could call anyone to touch bases.

My brother Ted and brother-in-law Bob usually hung out together, frequenting the sports bar and grilled steak counter with my brother Max. The charbroiled steak counter was the highlight of the cruise for them since all three were true steak lovers. Ted was the humorous and funny sports enthusiast. He was tickled to purchase an unlimited coke voucher for the week. Bob, on the other hand, was his own unique character. Deep down, he's compassionate and empathetic. He's not prone to giving compliments and does not outwardly show his caring nature. Instead, he resorts to highlighting others' inequities and dubbing people with negative nicknames such as "Useless," "Dumbbell," "Lowlife," or "One-Watt." But he is a caring individual and displays that quality only to those he cares about. If you were fortunate to be dubbed Useless or One-Watt, you knew you were one of his chosen few.

My other brother Jim is the two-year-old described in my Dedication. He was with my mother as she courageously diverted the Japanese soldiers when they came looking for my father after he escaped the Death March during World War II.

Jim was a life-long soldier, serving in the U.S. Army for 21 years. He is a proud American and proud to have served in the cause of freedom for his country. During his service, he was awarded many medals of valor and honor. Jim was away from our family for most of his military service period. During this time of absence from family, he and his wife Poppy had developed a very close bond of love and affection for one another, each being the other's main support through many years of difficult relocations, adjustments to new surroundings and cultures, health issues, multiple separations for interim service in the fields, and normal active military duty hardships. Consequently, during this luxurious cruise, he chose to enjoy more of his time with his wife and best friend, rather than venture off with the "other boys."

* * * * *

On one of the sea days, we planned a small get-together in two of my brothers' adjoining cabins so we could open the common door to the cabins.

I had brought some Portuguese Vinho Verde wine and some cans of nuts and other snacks, and we all had a great time one afternoon enjoying one another on a nice, lazy day. (This type of gathering was a tradition we adopted on our subsequent family reunion cruises.)

At dinner every night, we would all gather at our assigned tables and enjoy dinner together, sharing our day's experiences. One of us (I think it was me) decided to request a birthday cake for a couple of birthdays during our cruise. Then we got a little carried away and decided to celebrate different birthdays each night regardless of the fact that the birthdays were not during the duration of this cruise. But it was fun and festive, and each night we got a birthday cake with candles to blow out. Our waiters were very good-natured about our silliness and went right along with us, singing "Happy Birthday" as they appeared with a candlelit cake following dinner every evening. Our family truly enjoyed this aspect of our cruise.

We had a beautiful family portrait taken with all the siblings and spouses, with my aunt (whom we dubbed the matriarch of our family) front and center. She cherished that photo until she died, keeping an enlargement of it on her fireplace mantel. She boasted to her friends and other relatives about that cruise and how we five siblings had revered her as the matriarch of our family, as commemorated in the family portrait we had taken on the cruise. Her solo photo taken on that cruise was displayed during her subsequent funeral.

This was a wonderful, memorable reunion, enjoyed by all. We all agreed to follow with more reunion cruises every two years, sailing the Caribbean and Southern Caribbean, inviting other friends and other extended family; with our fourth and last cruise sailing the Mediterranean on a round-trip from Rome to Dubrovnik, Venice, Naples, Messina, Pisa (also visiting Florence), Cannes, and Barcelona, with a return to Rome, where we stayed for two or three more days before returning home. We later wanted to repeat this cruise, but the itinerary was no longer available. We were thrilled to have been able to take advantage of such a varied, interesting, and fun itinerary, as it was our last family reunion cruise together.

I will always be thankful that God gave me the idea for our first family reunion cruise and that we followed through for a total of four family reunion cruises over seven years while all us siblings were still alive here on earth.

27

About Gordy

*M*y firstborn nephew, radio announcer/DJ Gordy died on May 24, 2017. Gordy, the vibrant "Boomer Cruz," had been a renowned, exciting, resonating and energetic voice to millions of his listeners as a radio announcer and DJ in many areas of the San Francisco Bay Area, North Bay and Sacramento areas, including KSRY "Star FM" San Francisco; KFGY "Froggy" 92.9 (Country) Santa Rosa; KROY (Rock) V101, Sacramento, KHYL V101.1 Sacramento; KKIS "Kiss FM" Concord; KCRK "The Creek" Walnut Creek; KTOM (Country), V107FM and V109FM Salinas, and others. More recently, he became a mobile DJ, providing music and entertainment for various functions such as weddings, reunions, anniversaries, and the like. He was very professional and had a somewhat lucrative business, which had expanded mainly from referrals by satisfied customers. He always knew the right selection of music to play, tailored to his clients' requests. I miss my nephew immensely. He also was my reliable airport service, picking me up and dropping me off, even in the wee hours of the morning and late nights during my numerous and frequent trips back and forth between Sacramento and New York for many years.

*****

My sister and I (and I believe others) became more aware of how Gordy had become quite a benevolent close confidant, counselor, and friend to so many in the latter part of his life, having apparently become very sensitive, compassionate, and empathetic to others' problems and adverse circumstances. As we listened to the eulogies, experiences, thoughts, and stories shared by so many, we experienced a newfound awareness of the kind, sensitive, compassionate, caring, and empathetic nature of Gordy's character in later life. The celebration of Gordy's life the week following the funeral displayed a record attendance of so many who came to honor his life and accomplishments and to share their stories and remembrances of Gordy.

Rather than go on here to describe Gordy's life, I have included a very poignant eulogy given by myself. It expresses and highlights very important points about Gordy and his character and a very enlightening tale of Gordy from his early years.

Eulogy for Gordy, Saturday, June 3, 2017—
From your loving Aunt Vee

First of all, there's something highly amiss here. I was supposed to leave this life before Gordy, because Gordy was charged with playing my favorite Elvis gospel songs and ballads at my wake when I died. I am deeply saddened that not only will Gordy not be able to do this for me, but sad that I won't see him again until I am called.

Music was Gordy's love, and he enjoyed recording music for me that he pulled from his immense music library. I enjoyed hearing my favorite songs over and over again, even as many as ten times at once. Gordy got a kick out of that quirk of mine, as does my nephew Kenny. I would ask Gordy to record a favorite song for me, and he knew exactly what to do. Gordy knew his aunt was crazy, and he was quite amused every time I'd ask him to record a specific song several times on a disc. Once when my sister and I were riding on the highway, we were playing one of my special request CDs that Gordy had recorded. Elvis's "How Great Thou Art" and "Help Me" came on the player, and Val, who was driving, asked me to hurry and replay the two songs before moving on to the next. I told her to just wait, and on came the two songs again—and again. Val laughed when I told her Gordy had recorded this special disc for me with only these two favorite songs repeating over and over again. She laughed and said she would ask Gordy to record one for her as well. So we each have our own copies of our Gordy-recorded Elvis disc.

*****

What can I say about my firstborn nephew?

Gordy was such a happy, loving, jovial child, smart and quick-witted; he displayed a sharp intelligence. He was readily moved by music and a catchy tune. I remember at around age three, at Mom and Dad's house, when he heard the Batman theme, he danced around the living room singing "Na na na na na na na na Batman." He remained a Batman fan throughout his life, even as an adult.

Especially as a young child, I and many of our family were quite amused with Gordy. Even later in life, Gordy enjoyed hearing my stories of his childhood. He would laugh at the silly and witty things he had come up with, and then he'd ask me to tell the story again. I would like to share some of those stories with you, and I'm sure he'll be happy hearing and sharing them with you as well.

I remember one time, Gordy observed Grandpa in a quiet, pensive, troubled mood. Gordy asked him, "Grandpa, do you have problems?"

Grandpa said, "Yes, I've got problems."

Gordy replied, "Well, call the Roto-Rooter Man!"

And that got Grandpa laughing and laughing and out of his solemn mood.

One day when Gordy was about three years old, he and I were going downtown. I was buzzing around the house getting ready to go as little Gordy followed me around, observing my every move and watching me intently. I ran down the stairs to go see if I could see the bus coming.

As I got down to the bottom of the stairs, Gordy came running after me to the top of the stairs. He called after me, "Auntie, Auntie, you forgot something."

I said, "What?"

He said with a big smile on his face as he stretched out his arms and then pointed to himself, "You forgot *me*."

It was the cutest, most adorable gesture. But mean old Aunt Vee replied, "No, I didn't—you're not coming." It was so mean of me; of course, I was teasing.

But his crying face came on; his mouth turned from a smile down to a frown; his sparkling eyes welled with tears; and the poor little thing was so hurt, he began to wail and cry as tears flowed down his cheeks.

I ran up the stairs, grabbed him, and hugged him tight and told him, "Of course you're coming with me, honey; I'm so sorry."

And in an instant he was so happy and smiling again, with his two dimples showing, and wiped his tears as he bounced down the stairs with me. That was so mean of me, and I regretted having been so thoughtless.

Another time, at about the same age, Gordy and I must have gone downtown again, as we were transferring from the streetcar to the bus at Ocean Avenue and Junipero Serra. We were waiting in that little waiting shed until the bus came. Gordy told me he had to go to the bathroom. I said to him that we'd be home soon and maybe he could wait. I went to sit down. All of a sudden I looked up and saw him facing the cars passing by on Junipero Serra, which is quite a busy street. From his stance, I was horrified at what I thought he might be doing. I ran after him, and sure enough, this little three-year-old was urinating into the street, facing the passing cars. At that point, the cars were stopped at a red light. I said—dumb me—"Gordy, what are you doing? You can't do that!"

To which he replied, "Auntie, when I say I have to go, I have to go!" And that was that! He had taken it upon himself to solve the problem that his Aunt Vee couldn't solve. Well, what did I know? I was a very young teen!

Gordy and I took a lot of jaunts together when he was little. Most recently, Gordy would pick me up at the airport when I arrived from New York and take me back, picking me up to catch an early-morning six o'clock or six-thirty flight back. He never hesitated to pick me up at four or four fifteen to catch that flight. We always made a point to have lunch or dinner together before I would head back out, so we could do a little catch-up. It was very painful to me that he was not here this trip to do this for me. My last trip in February, our ritual changed, since I flew in and out of Oakland instead of Sacramento. My sister Val and brother-in-law Bob picked me up from the airport and brought me to stay with them in Vallejo. I had to drive about an hour and a half to Sacramento from Vallejo in a heavy storm to take care of something there. When I called Gordy and told him that because of the storm I wanted to turn right around and go back to Vallejo, he said he would come and meet me anywhere I wanted, so we could have our little session. When we parted, he said he was always so sad to see me leave, and his bear hug was a little tighter and longer. I'm so glad he pushed for our last lunch together.

Yes, Gordy had a strong love of family and of his close associates and friends. He was a very caring, compassionate individual, and I, and we, will all miss seeing him again here on earth. But he's in a wonderful place now and at peace.

We love you and miss you immensely, Gordy. Now, rest in peace.

28

The Closing of a Famous, Landmark Deli (and a Memoir of Ted)

For love of and in honor of my brother Ted, I went to the closing of a famous deli on December 30, 2016. I cannot ever remember in my lifetime standing and waiting in line for the better part of six hours. This was a first, and I'm quite sure an experience never again to be repeated by me. I just wanted to honor the memory of my brother and his visit to New York City years ago.

Friday, December 30, 2016

At four thirty in the morning, I was having breakfast of scrambled eggs, kidney beans, and ham in front of the TV, which was tuned to Channel 1 News for local news of New York. An announcement came on that this was the last day for business for a famous deli near the Times Square area. This landmark deli was due to close its doors for good at the end of business today. At hearing this news, I recalled that when my brother Ted was here in New York some ten years earlier, he, Val, and I went to this deli at Ted's request, since he had learned from his friend Charlotte that this was a "must visit" while in New York. So Ted, Val, and I sought out the C Deli and shared two humongous pastrami sandwiches. Many times since, when in the Times Square area, I attempted to get back to the deli but never quite made it. I guessed my plans for the day were about to change.

Earlier, I had planned to go to Bart's Trading to do some holiday shopping for my New Year's Eve celebration. Years ago when I first moved to New York, I tried to get someone to come to Times Square with me on New Year's Eve. To my disappointment, no one I knew would go with me because everyone said it was too crazy down there. But I, too, began to adopt that attitude. So I established a tradition of sitting at home in my apartment on New Year's Eve with a lavish spread of hors d'oeuvres, deli meats, and gourmet food and snacks, which I would begin dipping into sometime between eight and nine o'clock, along with a couple of bottles of champagne, which I would try to sip very slowly while waiting for the ball to drop on TV. Then I would get on the phone with my various friends and family in New York and California, and we would get caught up on the latest events of the year while we waited to ring in the New Year. This became a great tradition with my friends, because no one had to leave home, and we could get drunk as we yakked on the phone and just pass out at home if needed. Much of the time, unfortunately, I wouldn't last until the New Year and would likely be awakened by someone calling me from California on New York time to ring in the New Year. Anyway, I had planned to do my New Year's Eve shopping at Bart's Trading that day, among other errands to run. But first, I had to sit in the car until eleven thirty in the morning to wait for the street sweeper to come and go.

When I heard the news of the deli closing this day, I really wanted to go in honor of Ted and my memory of our lunch together with him, my sister, and me years ago. I would also bring my camera and take pictures of the inside of the deli where we sat, to put in my picture album. Anyway, I could also purchase some great pastrami for my feast tomorrow. So after the street sweeper chore, I dropped off my reading materials in my apartment and then headed out to the C Deli. When I got off the bus, I took pictures of the outside of the deli from across the street and from the side streets. Then I noticed the long line of people going down the block and rounding the corner. There were two lines, for eat-in and for takeout, so I got in the takeout line. *(Surely the takeout line should move along, even though it was a long line.)* I couldn't believe that I might be waiting for two to three hours to gain entry.

After two hours, I took stock and tried to decide whether or not to continue waiting. The lines were so slow; no one seemed to be moving. *I knew I had to be absolutely nuts to be doing this, waiting for hours on end to get into a restaurant, but my heart tugged at me to do this for Ted, so I could enjoy the special pastrami one more time for him and be able to take pictures of the inside of the restaurant where we once sat.* Well, I continued to wait. Snow began to fall, quite heavily, intermittently, but fortunately for us deli patrons, there was an overhead scaffolding above us that shielded us from the falling snow. After about three and a half hours of waiting, I decided to go to a coffeehouse on the corner to buy a cup of coffee and to use their restroom. *Wrong!* There was no restroom facility at this location. So after I got back, I talked with the agent at the entry door to the deli and asked to be admitted to use their restroom facilities. This doorman was so pleasant: "Of course you may come in to use the restroom." So I went in and went to the ladies' room and also took pictures where I remembered Val, Ted, and I had sat when we had lunch. I also was able to take pictures of the entire dining room and the entire deli counter with all the photos of visiting celebrities on all the walls. Quite relieved and happy that I had all my pictures, I went back into the line.

After about four and a half hours in line, one of the ladies I had been waiting with, whose daughter was in the dine-in line, was called in for a party of two. Meanwhile, I had about another forty-five minutes to one hour to wait to gain entry. I had been in line since a quarter to three in the afternoon. Finally, at close to eight o'clock, I was allowed to enter the restaurant (a total of about five hours and fifteen minutes after entering the waiting line). Well, once inside, there was another line to place your order. It was another forty-five minutes for my order to be filled, and I could finally leave.

I got home at nine thirty with all my goodies. Then I ate and enjoyed some as I reminisced about Ted with me and my sister enjoying those humongous pastrami sandwiches at the deli so many years ago. I saved some for my New Year's Eve feast the next day, and then I repacked the remainder of my goods in smaller freezable packets to enjoy slowly at later times.

Despite the ridiculously long wait, I felt good having done this for Ted. To be sure, I have never in my life before, nor probably would ever again after this, wait in line for five and a quarter hours and a total of almost six hours to gain entry into a restaurant and complete my order.

*****

This whole fiasco was only to honor my deceased brother Ted. I miss him terribly. I miss his smile, his quick wit and spontaneity, his amusing and humorous personality, which would bring laughter to those around. He exuded a generous sharing and caring nature, which he even imparted to his feral cats, always ensuring they were fed.

We all miss Ted at our family gatherings. Ted was such an avid sports fan. Several times around his birthday, he vacationed in Hawaii just to attend the Pro Bowl. He was also fortunate to hold season tickets for the San Francisco Giants and 49er games. Apparently when the new sports field was being built in San Francisco, Ted took a daily ride to the construction site to view its progress. When the Giants won the World Series in 2012, Ted and Gordy, and other nephews, nieces, brothers, and Ted's many friends and Giants fans, were absolutely elated and jubilant. Their jubilance continued for days thereafter.

Sports were a priority during family get-togethers; game times could not be interrupted, whether just a normal weekend or during Thanksgiving and holiday celebrations. The room would be filled with excitement and anticipation as all watched the games.

We miss Ted immensely at our campouts at Donner Lake, where our family and friends gathered annually for nearly thirty years to enjoy three days and nights in the refreshing mountain air among the pines, the lake, and just good old-fashioned camaraderie as we'd roast marshmallows, sing around the campfire, and share jokes and stories of bygone days. I can smell the early morning aromas of grilled bacon, eggs and pancakes, and freshly brewed coffee, avidly prepared by chefs Ted, Max, and Bob. Ted had taken on the responsibility of ensuring that the campouts continued annually without interruption for so many years. Consequently, we have many, many years of memories of good wholesome outdoor fun and eats and a tradition of sharing.

Mostly, we all just miss Ted, his smile and his laugh, his amusing, quick-witted, and humorous personality, and his sensitive, thoughtful, compassionate, and empathetic nature.

My love for him and missing his presence are all that allowed me to complete this day in this manner. *This one was for you, Ted!*

29
Analogy of Life and Death

As I stated in my introduction:

Life is like a stream flowing down a mountain. It flows over pebbles, reeds, twigs, rocks, and small branches as it continues on down the mountain. The river meanders downstream, hitting and flowing around the obstacles in its way. It comes across larger branches, larger rocks, and big logs and continues to circumvent them as it continues downstream. It hits larger tree trunks and small boulders and continues to flow around them and the myriad of obstructions as it continues its journey, flowing and meandering its way downward. Suddenly, it hits a huge boulder and flows around the boulder until it finally reaches a calm, placid lake at the bottom of the mountain, surrounded by the beauty of majestic mountains, where it basks in the warmth of the sun and the beauty of its serene surroundings.

*****

As posed in my analogy above, we all must deal with our share of pain and unhappiness throughout our lifetimes. I believe how we survive the obstacles of life and push forward through the untoward circumstances we encounter throughout life are a result of what and how we learn from those untoward experiences and implement changes in our attitudes as a result of those experiences. My theory is to look at life after those instances with a more positive attitude, trying to sort out the truly grave and serious circumstances from the less serious and treat them accordingly. Glean a little humor and purpose in the various occurrences of life when appropriate, and go forth with as much ease as your individual constitution allows.

* * * *

As you read this book, there are many events that took place. How I handled the situations may likely seem to most to have been ridiculously handled and most likely overstated, enhanced, or totally made up, because no one would be crazy or ridiculous enough to do as I did.

Let me say that I have been driven to do things and handle situations as I did, not to prove a point to anyone or even to myself, but because I felt I was physically and mentally able to do them and was grateful that I, in fact, was physically, mentally, and emotionally able to handle those situations. After having battled cancer twice and seemingly survived, and then contracting the condition of rheumatoid arthritis, a very debilitating disease or condition, in addition to surviving shingles and an almost three-hour awake surgery, I felt, and still feel, very fortunate with the grace of God to be able to do as I have done. I feel that as long as I am mentally and physically able to function as I have been doing, I will continue to do so, because I ought not to accept my limitations and inadequacies outright as an excuse to just continue to deteriorate without persevering/pushing forth to accomplish tasks that I am able to pursue and accomplish.

30
Philosophies and Inner Thoughts (and Loss of Loved Ones)

Nostalgia is a memory of days gone by. It can bring warmth and joy in the remembrance, or it can bring sadness and hollowness in the reflection of a painful memory.

I do believe that who we are and become throughout various stages of our lives is shaped a great deal by our experiences and the people with whom we become acquainted or with whom we spend time or share our lives. What we hear and experience and how we analyze, learn from, educate ourselves, and incorporate changes in our behavior and thinking as a result are important elements in shaping our character as we go through life. I believe most healthy people change their character to some degree at various points throughout their lifetimes, unfortunately many times because of uncontrollable life experiences, such as health issues of self or loved ones, their individual personal circumstantial changes, social changes, and most profoundly by experiencing death of a loved one.

In the case of myself, the experience of losing to death my baby brother Ted, my ex-husband Tim, and my firstborn DJ and radio announcer nephew Gordy, three of my closest and most beloved relatives in a short consecutive three-plus years' time, caused profound changes in my emotional being and resulted in a very diminished degree of excitement, anticipation, and joy I now feel regarding positive events in my current life. After the death of my brother Ted, the first of the three to die, the excruciating emotional pain that followed still lives within me, and I have since lost my passion for living. I no longer am as outgoing and carefree as I had been lucky to be all the years of my life prior to his death.

The added recent loss of my brother Jim, the two-year-old companion of my mother during World War II when Japanese soldiers came looking for my father who escaped the Death March, demonstrates the increasing painful experiences we all face in our life's journey.

The outcome of my serious illnesses (more completely explained in my opening chapters), which were such traumatic experiences and resulted in my physical impairment, affected my character in a more positive, meaningful outward look on life. The experience and finality of the recent deaths of four of my beloved relatives have forced me to reach even deeper within my being for the strength necessary to go forth in life and have deeply affected me and my character.

It is unfortunate that in each instance, I learned more about each of them after their deaths, mostly by hearing from others whose lives they had affected, of the compassion, empathy, and understanding they had each shared with so many, many people outside of their immediate families. Each of them had extended their families ten- and twenty-fold in the very close personal relationships they nurtured in addition to their biological families.

I so wish that I had spent more time while they were alive to learn and know more about them. However, one thing I do now understand about each of them is that although they did so much good for so many others in their earthly lifetimes, they each were very humble in performing those wonderful deeds. Not one of them had ever boasted about all the good deeds they performed, the compassion and empathy they had shared with so many. They each performed those deeds out of the goodness of their hearts, not ever expecting to be applauded for them. Since their deaths, I have gained a better understanding of each of their lives, how they lived and thought, and what they each accomplished in their lifetimes.

When I think of any of them, the wave of nostalgia is so profound—a sweet, bitter reflection and deep sadness that I had not known their true characters until I lost them to death.

* * * * *

I have experienced a life-altering lesson, which I believe many people learn following the death of a loved one. *I believe a common thread in the loss of a loved one is that most survivors feel and wish they had spent more quality time with and/or learned more about the decedent.* Often there is an agonizing realization that thoughts and words meant for the decedent now must remain unspoken, a remorseful wish that one had taken the time to express those thoughts to the decedent prior to the death of the loved one. The stark awareness that the opportunity to utter those words to the deceased loved one has passed and is no longer possible becomes very real, and the hollowness of that realization leaves an excruciating and gnawing, aching pain and thread of regret for the loss of opportunity to utter those words to the loved one nevermore. This pain and agony lives on, and hopefully, with the forgiving passage of time, the pain becomes diminished.

* * * * * *